INTRODUCTION

Since the pages of this book was digitalized from a very old original,
the pages here may look a little funny at times.
Rest assured we did our best to format the original book
into modern form as best allowed by the current processes available.

Although each page of this book was copied from the original edition,
this reprint is in no way endorsed by or associated with "The Only William".

Ross Brown

Introduction and Cover Art Copyright 2008 -
All rights reserved.

For regular updates on new reprint editions of
vinatge cocktail books,
vintage wine books,
vintage drinks books and
vintage cooking books
please visit

www.VintageCocktailBooks.com

THE FLOWING BOWL

WHEN AND WHAT TO DRINK

BY
THE ONLY WILLIAM
(William Schmidt)

FULL INSTRUCTIONS HOW TO PREPARE, MIX,
AND SERVE BEVERAGES

New York:
CHARLES L. WEBSTER & CO.
1892

COPYRIGHT, 1891,
BY
WILLIAM SCHMIDT.
(*All rights reserved.*)

PRESS OF
JENKINS & McCOWAN,
NEW YORK.

Contents.

	PAGE
HISTORY	17–38
Wine	19
Beer	23
Alcohol	28
Coffee	31
Tea	33
Water	35
Mineral Water	38
PHYSIOLOGY AND DIET	39–47
COMPOSITION OF DRINKS AND THEIR ADULTERATIONS	49–64
Water	52
Milk	55
Wine	57
Beer	61
Spirits	63
ETHNOGRAPHY	65
OUR ANCESTORS	73
Description of a Greek Banquet	75
Description of a Roman Banquet (*Prose*)	77
Description of a Roman Banquet (*Poetry*)	82
A Royal Feast Among the Huns	86
A Menu of Emperor Charles V	88
WHAT KINDS OF WINES AND IN WHICH ORDER SHOULD THEY BE SERVED AT A REPAST?	91
SAMPLE MENUS	95

CONTENTS.

	PAGE
INTRODUCTION TO MIXED DRINKS	105

CONTAINING HINTS TO THE PROFESSIONAL BARKEEPER AND GENERAL REMARKS TO THE PUBLIC.

MIXED DRINKS	121
SOURS	123
COCKTAILS	125
PUNCHES (FOR THE BAR USE)	131
LEMONADES	135
TEMPERANCE DRINKS	137
COBBLERS	144
FIZZES	145
DIVERSE	147
LIQUORS AND RATAFIAS	179
PUNCHES	209
BOWLS	237
KALTSCHALEN (BISHOPS)	249
EXTRA DRINKS	255
FRUIT WINES	261
POETRY	273

Preface.

WHILE having been active for a period of more than thirty years in the line of hotel and bar business, and having given my greatest care to mixed drinks particularly, I have found them to be great favorites among connoisseurs.

Repeatedly the desire has been expressed to me as to where to obtain satisfactory and reliable information how to prepare such delicious mixtures. A great number of men received such information from me, as far as a few minutes' conversation could teach anybody.

The oftener, however, such questions were repeated, the more established became within me the conviction that there was among the public a general desire for a book containing all advices of such a kind. The result of this conviction is this book, that hereby is handed over to the public.

Feeling that I had to place on the market only a first-class manual, in all its details and instructions, I have given it the most particular care and study. Utmost diligence and attention have assisted me to express my thoughts in clear and exact terms, so as to enable any one, even private persons, to understand and comprehend how to obtain the most satisfactory results.

I might compare mixing drinks with the working in

fractions, especially in circulating decimals; if we are not very careful in the order in which we do certain operations, we most certainly will never arrive at a correct result; neglecting following decimal places will largely affect the correctness of our final answer. So, too, in mixing drinks: The fractional parts of liquors that are to be mixed, and their order, have to be carefully considered, and without such consideration no palatable drink may be expected.

I do not deny that a book on drinks will mainly have to cover the demands of public resorts, but I hope, and I am sure many join me in this feeling, that there will be a time when reasonable drinking is not looked upon as a crime; and the time will come when around the table the whole family sits chatting and whiling idle hours away, while the sparkling bowl sharpens their wit and loosens their tongues; when father and grown-up sons will not leave their homes to seek recreation, but when they will spend their leisure time in the family circle.

By careful investigation every impartial reader will find that nearly all recipes concerning bowls, punches, etc., are made not so much for the bar-use as for the family.

It may sound strange from the lips of a mixer of drinks, and still it is the truth—*I believe in temperance.* Surely this my belief has no reference to temperance that identifies itself with prohibition, but it has reference to temperance in the word's true meaning: tempering or moderating the enjoyment of liquors.

A habitual drinker will never indulge in beverages artistically mixed; he lacks the taste of them, as they do not bring him rapidly enough to his desired nirvana. In drinking, our aim must be enjoyment, not inebriation. Thus the culture of mixed drinks will lead us with greater sureness to true temperance than all blue laws ever will be able to do.

Another reason for setting my foot upon the slippery road of a public writer was the general approval my new concoctions met with. For years I have been urged to publish the recipes of the same; some of them have been communicated to the public by the medium of our leading newspapers, when occasion and demand seemed to render it desirable. Never, however, I felt inclined to giving the reader only a series of recipes. My ambition took a higher flight. If ever I was to place anything upon the market, it should be a book containing not only recipes valuable to professional men mostly, but one, the reading matter of which should be of a kind that every intelligent man might find at least something to arouse his interest. Should this my sincere wish find fulfillment, even in a limited degree, my labor bestowed on this volume I should not think wasted.

The reading matter does not claim to replace an encyclopædia; I restrained myself to select only such subjects as might be of some value to the majority of my readers. In the Physiology of Drinking I preferred to give general hints than an entire treatise on this subject, which, treated upon extensively, would by itself fill a volume similar to this in size. The pages about poetry, likewise, give only a selection of the best poets: should I have omitted one of the favorites of my esteemed readers, I beg their kind forgiveness.

The drinks themselves are divided into two great groups, such as served and serviceable at the bar only, which are enumerated under the heading "Mixed Drinks," and such as might be desirable for societies and larger companies, as punches, bowls, etc.

While thanking my co-workers for their kind and indefatigable assistance, and expressing my heartfelt gratitude to my many patrons for the interest they took in the book while it still was unwritten, as well as to Messrs. Chas. L. Webster & Co. for the care which they bestowed upon the outfit of same, I deliver these pages to the public.

May it be accompanied by kindness, and may it, in return, be a guide to the reader that will show him the path to many a happy hour.

Very respectfully yours,

A. WILLIAM SCHMIDT.

History.

Wine.

ASIA is undoubtedly the country where the vine has grown without the helping hand of man, and very probably the slopes south of the Caucasus, where still nowadays, as in the Kolchian forest, the vine grows in abundance and richness.

Elphinstone—born 1778, died 1859—on his journey to Cabul, saw in the Caucasian forests the vine growing wild, and describes how fascinating to the eye the entanglement and coverings of whole forests by the vine appeared. Modern travelers report of bunches of grapes of seventeen pounds in Palestine, and of a vinetree on the southern slope of the Lebanon Mountains, the diameter of which was one foot and a half; it was thirty feet high, and formed, by its twigs and boughs, a canopy of two hundred feet in circumference. In the vicinity of Naples you may see vines, the stems of which are only a little thinner than the trees to which they cling. As to the size of grapes, they are naturally larger under the glowing sun of the south. Already in Italy we see exceedingly large bunches; still larger they are found in Greece and Asia Minor. Near Shiraz, in Persia, their length amounts to a yard. Baron De Huegel found them of colossal size in Cashmere.

Lady Sale, in her memoirs from Afghanistan, speaks of grapes of which a single berry weighed one hundred and twenty-nine grains.

The mythology of the Greeks mentions the birth of Dionysos, or Bacchus—or what is identical to both, the home of the vine—as taking place upon the mountain Nysa, a peak of the Hindoo Koosh, an Indian chain of the gigantic Himalaya system.

This god was brought up by mountain-nymphs, and educated by the muses, fauns, the old Silen, and the satyrs; in harmony with this education his worshipers represented him as a bewitching youth, with forms resembling woman, and with gladness on his brow, or as adorned with vine-wreaths, resting among beautiful women, who, singing and dancing, give us the prettiest and oldest allegory of "Wine, Wife, and Song."

He is also represented as rambling over wide fields, drawn by panthers.

In a different light appears the vine in the history of the Jews, but also here, in closest connection with their elder father; Noah's wine soon became a favorite beverage among the Hebrews, who were anything but teetotalers.

When the Israelites left Egypt to return to their old country, Canaan, explorers, sent out, brought back a huge bunch of grapes, the best proof for the wine-culture in Palestine at this early time, 1250 B. C.

The travels of Bacchus allegorically allude to the spreading of the wine-culture from east to west.

According to the myth, it took its way over Arabia, Egypt, and Libya to Hellas; later on to Italy, and finally to Spain and Gaul.

The worship of Bacchus was corresponding to the importance of the wine-culture, and found its acme in the Dionysians of the Greeks, and the Bacchanals of the Romans.

Historical traditions call the Phœnicians the first wine-growers; they brought the vine to the islands of Chios, Mitylene, and Tenedos.

Already, in the year 550 B. C., the process of blending selected wines was known to the Carthaginians.

Herodotus and Theophrastus give accounts of the Egyptian wine-culture, which has long since died out.

The ancient Persia produced the precious royal wine of Chalybon, and the valuable brands of Bactriana, Ariana, Hyrkania, and Margiana.

In India the priests, and in Egypt the priests and kings, were forbidden to drink, while the Jewish priests were only prohibited on days of religious services.

Homerus many times mentions the wine as sorrow-breaking and heart-refreshing, and as a beverage for the gods.

In Italy wine was first cultivated in Campania. The most celebrated wines of ancient Italy were: Falernian, Faustinian, Caecubian, Massician, Setinian, and those of Formia, Calene, etc.

The old custom of adding turpentine to the wine, for the purpose of preserving, was followed also in Italy;

hence the resemblance of the tip of a Thyrsus-staff to the cone of a pine.

The wine-production of the old Romans was enormous; Cæsar presented to the city of Rome at one single time 44,000 barrels; Hortensius had not less than 10,000 barrels of extra Chios wine in his cellars.

Gaul (France) was a wine-growing country long before Germany, as already, 600 B. C., the Phocians in Massilia, the modern Marseilles, introduced the wine here.

Cæsar already found in Gaul extensive vineyards; Ausonius praises the wines of Medoc; Plinius those of the Auvergne.

Emperor Domitian ordered half of the Gallic vineyards to be destroyed, and in their stead that grain should be raised; this would have the double effect of reducing the price of the grain, and of securing better prices to the wine-growers in Italy.

Emperor Probus revoked this edict. Aurelian and the Antonines planted vines in the Côté d'Or, the best product of which is still nowadays called "Romanée."

Charlemagne owned vineyards in Burgundy, and brought the vine from there to the Rhine.

In exchange for thirty barrels of Chambertin the abbot of Citeaux received from Pope Gregory IX. the dignity of cardinal.

During the crusades French pilgrims brought eastern vines to France.

The sparkling champagne was not known yet at the

close of the seventeenth century, as its invention was made by Dom Perignon, of Hautvillers, during the time from 1670–1715.

In the sixteenth century the German wine-grower, Peter Simon, took the vine from the Rhine to Malaga, which now supplies us with the most delicious wine.

But it would take us too long, and it would very likely become annoying to our kind readers, to go further into details; only this must not be suppressed, that America's first discoverers, the Northmen, found ripe grapes in 1000 A. D., and named the unknown shore Vinland, a place supposed to be on the coast of Massachusetts. But the proper cultivation of wine in the United States reaches back not farther than to the beginning of this century.

Beer.

"BEER is a light, narcotic, alcoholic beverage, which charms us into a state of gladness and soft hilarity; it protects our hearts against stings of all kinds, awaiting us in this valley of misery; it diminishes the sensitiveness of our skin to the nettles and to all the bites of the numberless, detestable human insects that hum, hiss, and hop about us.

"The happy mortal who has selected beer as his preferred stimulant imbeds greater griefs and joys in soft pillows; surely thus being wrapped up he will be able to travel through this stormy life with less danger.

"Yes, I find such a perfection of forms, such a softness and ductility of the tissue in the pale juice of barley, that I, to express its physiology with a few words, might say: 'It is to us in our lifetime like a wrapper which enables our fragile nature unendangered to reach the safe port.'"

This quotation is a verbatim translation from a book, *The Hygiena of Taste*, by the world-famous Italian physician and physiologist, Paolo Montegazza.

Nobody will to-day declare that Lager, as we usually call it, has not had the greatest influence upon the development of nations, especially those of German descent.

We do not mean Germans proper of the present time, but all those nations that trace their origin back to the German tribes that wandered, during the fourth and fifth centuries, over the entire part of Europe, and even crossed the Strait of Gibraltar into Africa.

Yet we would be mistaken to believe that beer was unknown to the ancients.

Sophocles and Æschylos, those famous Greek tragedians, Diodorus of Sicily, Pliny, the greatest representative of natural philosophy of Roman times, and others, already mention the beer (in Greek, *zythos*).

Famous breweries were at Pelusium in lower Egypt, the Beeropolis of the ancients, as nowadays are Munich in the Old, and New York, St. Louis, and Milwaukee in the New World.

The Egyptians made their beer from barley. The secrets of brewing after Egyptian prescriptions were imported into the south and north of Europe by the Phenicians. Greeks, Romans, and Gauls enjoyed their lager: the Romans called it, uniformly with the Gauls, Cerevisia, from Ceres, the goddess of field fruits. The old Saxons and Danes were extremely fond of it, and counted drunkenness from it as one of the highest rewards awaiting them in Walhalla, their Paradise, where reside Odin's heroes.

An old German story has it that Gambrinus, king of Brabant, was the inventor of beer, and it is in consequence of this that the brewers revere this mythical king as their patron.

In Germany, beer was introduced at large during the twelfth and thirteenth centuries, although already six centuries ago we find the beer in Germany mentioned; we dare not omit the phrase of Tacitus in his Germania that the Suevians enjoyed a beverage made by fermentation of grain.

For instance, we find in a law collection of the Alemannians, a German tribe residing on both sides of the Rhine, from Basel to Mayence, the remark that every one belonging to any parish was obliged to give fifteen gallons of beer to the parson.

Charlemagne also here did not underestimate the value of it; for he called the best brewers to his court and also gave orders how to brew.

Since 1482, a heavy beer has been made in the monasteries of Germany; it was of two kinds, a better quality for the Fathers and a cheaper one for the convent.

In the sixteenth century, the brewing business of Germany ranked very high and beer was one of the chief exports of this country.

The Thirty Years' War destroyed this industry. The public prosperity faded and the quality, the reputation of the beer and the demand for it were likewise diminished.

Up to that time beer was made in smaller villages in every household; after it, especially in lower Germany and the Netherlands, a specific brewery business was created, which flourished mainly in Ghent, Brugge, and Brussels; Ratisbon and Ulm were the brewing centres of South Germany.

In cities where, on account of the lack of good cellars, etc., it was difficult to make good and palatable beer, the city authorities ordered beer in casks from abroad, and these were put on draught in public places, built expressly for this purpose.

All persons having visited the old country are aware of the existence of so-called "Rathskellers," as for instance in Bremen, Lubeck, Salzburg, etc. These cellars owe their origin to this arrangement of the city government; yet these public places changed afterward from beer into wine depositories.

Some beers of that time acquired a very great reputation, as those of Brunswick, Eimbeck, Merseburg, Bamberg, etc.

In England were the better beers, as ale and porter, not manufactured before the end of the last century; up to that time the English drank beer resembling the so-called "Convent Beer" of Germany.

In the second half of our century the breweries changed into beer factories. The increasing prosperity after the close of the Napoleonic wars and the foundation of duty-treaties between the different states increased the riches of the nations and were of enormous influence upon the quality and demand of beer.

At present the Bavarian beer is thought to be the best, and the methods followed there are accepted in the greater part of Europe—except England and the specific wine countries—in North America and Australia, nay, even in Turkey, the inhabitants of which country congratulate themselves that in Mohammed's time nothing was known concerning brewing, or Mohammed certainly would have prohibited his followers from enjoying this beverage as well as the wine.

Bismarck, "The Man of Blood and Iron," made once the remark: "Beer renders people stupid." But the same man did not hesitate to use and enjoy it himself, especially at his receptions of the members of the Reichstag in the Chancellor's Palace, and we still await reports that the use of beer has badly affected his mental capacities.

During the last three decades new rivals to the Bavarian beer have arisen in Austria, at Schwechat and at Pilsen, and last, but not least, in the great brewing centres of the New World.

The world-wide importance beer has won is best

illustrated by the different papers devoted expressly to brewing purposes, as: *The American Brewer*, New York; *Der Bierbrauer*, Chicago; *The Bavarian Brewer*, Munich; *The Beerbrewer*, Leipsic; *The Bohemian Beerbrewer*, Prague, and others.

Alcohol.

THE use of alcoholic beverages, such as wine, beer, etc., was known to most nations of ancient times, as we have seen above; but they were known only in regard to their effect upon the body. In respect to a fundamental knowledge of alcohol, the ancients were absolutely in the dark, as the distilling apparatuses of those times were too imperfect.

The philosophers of Alexandria are said to have distilled wine, and noticed the combustibility of the distillate.

We find the expression, *aqua vitæ*, or "water of life," that was afterward generally applied to alcohol, in the Latin translation of Geber's writings—eighth century; yet he does not mention anything about the chief characteristic of the fluid—its combustibility.

Since the thirteenth century this fluid has been used for medical purposes, and all alchemists and physicians tried to obtain it in the greatest possible concentration.

On this account distillations and rectifications were

made over and over again. Raimundus Lullus, born at Mallorca in the year 1234, suggested that the philosopher's stone, that would change all metals into real gold, might be won from the three natural kingdoms. To have it from plants, one had to begin with alcohol.

His theory of the preparation of the substance that was to become the philosopher's stone follows:

"*Accipe nigrum nigrius nigro et ex eo partes octodecim destilla in vase argenteo, aureo vel vitreo. Et in prima destillatione solum recipe partem primæ cum dimidia, et hanc partem iterum pone ad destillandum. Et hujus iterum quartam partem et tertio destilla et hujus recipe duas, et in quarta destillatione pauco minus quam totum. Et sic destilla illam partem usque ad octo vel novem vices, vel decies.*"

This distillate is afterward once more rectified over a very slow fire, during from twenty to twenty-two days: "*quanto destillatio ejus fuerit leviori igne, tanto subtilior erit in spiritu et fortitudine.*"

It is hardly worth while to state that Lullus did not find "the philosopher's stone." We know "Work is the true philosopher's stone that changes all metals into gold."

The notes of Lullus are, in many points, indistinct; much clearer are the remarks of Basilius Valentinus— fourteenth century. He recommends the use of carbonate of potassium; yet this was accepted much later. Pure alcohol was first manufactured according to this principle by Lowitz, in the year 1796, *i. e.*, more than four centuries later.

What we now call alcohol had, from the eleventh to the sixteenth century, very different names: *Aqua ardens, aqua vitæ, aqua vitæ ardens, aqua vini, spiritus vini, vinum ardens, mercurius vegetabilis,* etc. Since the beginning of the sixteenth century the name of "alcohol" was more and more adopted. It derives its name from the Arabian word "al-kohl," *i. e.*, a name of a fine powder with which the eyelashes are dyed, therefore a substance changed into the finest aggregation of molecules.

About the nature and composition of alcohol there were as many different meanings and opinions as there were writers, and each following more fantastic, if it were possible, than the previous one. But all these phantasmagories faded away like fog before the sun when the great French chemist, Lavoisier, inaugurated a new era in chemistry by his discovery of oxygen; he proved that the elementary parts of alcohol were carbon, hydrogen and oxygen.

Originally, it was used for medical purposes only; but gradually people found its effect upon the human body, and drank it, whether they were sick or not, because it worked more rapidly than wine and beer.

The general use of alcohol is of comparatively recent date—not before the fifteenth century we find in Europe the use of "*aqua vitæ*," together with that of wine and beer.

Coffee.

THE earlier history of the coffee-tree is rather obscure; the Greeks and Romans did not know it. Its fruits were used in Abyssinia and Nubia, in Arabia, since the fifteenth century, and in other countries of the Orient since the sixteenth century.

The application of coffee-beans for a beverage had its origin in Arabia, and spread from there in the sixteenth century to Egypt and Constantinople. Leonhard Rauwolf, a German physician, was likely the first that made the coffee known in Western Europe by the publication of his travels in the year 1573. In A. D. 1591 Prosper Alpinus brought some beans as a drug from Egypt to Venice.

Coffee was drunk in Italy already in the beginning of the seventeenth century, in France and England in the middle, and in Germany at the end, of the same century. A more general use of it, however, cannot be reported before the eighteenth century.

The first coffee-house in Europe was opened at Constantinople in the year 1551. A century later, in the year 1652, another one was opened in London at Newman's Court in Cornhill by a Greek servant of the merchant Edwards, whose ships sailed to and from the Levant. Paris saw its first café opened in the year 1670; it was owned by the Armenian Pascal. The next one in the same city was the Café Procope, established by the Sicilian Procopio, in the year 1725; it was frequented by all the literary men of France that visited Paris, and soon became fashionable, but also the meeting-place of republicans and revolutionists.

Vienna opened its first café in the year 1694; the privilege was granted to a Polish citizen for the services he had rendered when the capital was besieged by the Turks in the year 1683. Berlin received its first mocha-temple in the year 1721.

King Frederick I. of Prussia, an obstinate enemy of coffee, made the coffee-trade a monopoly; nobody but the clergy and the nobility were permitted to roast their own coffee. The people at large had to pay, in the royal roasting-houses, from six to seven times more than they would have paid at the merchant's.

In Leipsic the first coffee-house was opened to the public in the year 1694, in Stuttgart in the year 1712.

The infamous Jew Süss, founded in Wuertemberg a coffee-monopoly by granting the privilege of sale only to such people as were able and willing to pay him for it liberally.

The colonists that sailed out to find new islands and to found new settlements took the coffee-beans the decoction of which had become already a necessity with them. A mayor of Amsterdam, Wieser, is said to have brought the coffee-tree from Mocha to Batavia, where he established great plantations; this took place at the end of the seventeenth century. From Batavia he sent 169 young trees to Amsterdam for the Botanical Garden, whence the Jardin des Plantes in Paris received one. Captain Declieux took a layer of this to Martinique, where it grew so well that in a few years all the Antilles could be supplied with trees.

The consumption of coffee amounts, in England, to $1\frac{1}{3}$ lbs., in France to $2\frac{1}{2}$, in Germany to 4, in Denmark to $5\frac{1}{2}$, in Switzerland to 6, in Holland to 10 to 12, and in the United States to more than 9 lbs. per head yearly.

Tea.

TEA is the name of a shrub belonging to the *Camellia* family with alternate and simple leaves, not dotted; the flowers are large and showy, with a persistent calyx of five overlapping sepals, and they have many stamens, their filaments united at the bottom with each other and with the base of the petals.

Formerly different kinds were supposed to exist, all of which were said to be indigenous to China, Japan and India, until Robert Fortune, known by his botanical journeys, proved the incorrectness of this opinion. He lived for a long while in the tea districts of China and India for the purpose of studying the manufacture of tea; he showed that all sorts of tea that are thrown upon the market descend from one kind that extremely varies; this variation is shown chiefly in regard to the length and width of the leaves; in the course of a thousand years' cultivation a great number of varieties had sprung forth from this one kind. The tea shrub grows in its wild state 6 to 10 metres high; while the cultivated shrub reaches a height of not more than 2 metres, or 6 feet.

The cultivation of tea, according to Chinese traditions of the fourth century, came from Corea to China, and from there to Japan in the ninth century.

About the sixth century the Chinese used to drink tea nearly all over their country. The Europeans have tried to plant and cultivate the tea-shrub in Bengal, Ceylon, on the western coast of Africa, in Java and Sumatra, in Brazil, and many other places. In all these districts the shrub grows, but is degenerated detrimentally, as its aroma never reaches that of the genuine Chinese tea.

The method of extracting the *teïn* by boiling water has been known in China as long as the cultivation of the shrub; the Europeans, however, learned it very late, first by the Dutch East India Company, about the middle of the seventeenth century, although the first importation of tea to Europe had taken place already in the year 1636. England got its first tea in the year 1666. The consumption of it increased continually, and was general in the eighteenth century. Although tea was believed for a long while a sure and reliable drug for lengthening life, the habit of tea-drinking is not so widely spread as that of coffee.

Tea-drinking has become a national habit only

among the Dutch and the English, who imported the tea also to their colonies in North America, the United States, and Canada, to the Cape of Good Hope and to Australia, likewise to Portugal. Russia, Sweden, Norway, and the coast countries of middle Europe rank next.

Who does not know of the great tea-riot in Boston that gave the signal for the outbreak of the Revolution, and shows the importance tea had obtained at that time in a colonist's household?

Water.

WATER was believed to be an element from the very earliest times down to only a few decades ago.

Moses mentions, in the first chapter of his Genesis, water as one of the first created elementary bodies. The Hindoos and Egyptians regarded it the basis of most of the other bodies. Among the Greeks, Thales —600 B. C.—defended the opinion that water was the only true element, and that all other bodies, plants and animals included, were formed out of it.

Diodorus, about the year 30 B. C., suggested that rock-crystal developed from the purest water, not under the influence of cold, but under that of the heavenly fire. This opinion of the development of the stone, the characteristic ingredient of which is silex, is affirmed by its Greek name, *krystallos*, or ice.

Soon others got up and declared rock-crystal was not formed out of water by heat, but by long-lasting cold. Pliny, after he has spoken of solids and their formation out of warmth and cold, says:

"*Contraria huic causa crystallum facit, gelu vehementiore concreto. Non aliubi certe reperitur quam ubi maxime hibernæ nives rigent, glaciemque esse certum est, unde et nomen Græci dedere.*" Seneca Minor and other contemporaries express the same opinion, as does also Isodorus of the seventh century.

Agricola of the sixteenth century is the first philosopher who is opposed to it; in his book *De Ortu et Causis Subterraneorum* he says: "If the crystal was formed out of water, it naturally would have to be lighter than water, for ice floats on water. He denies emphatically that any stony material might be formed of water without any additional ingredients : "*Satis intellegimus, ex sola aqua non gigni lapidem ullum.*"

In the seventeenth century alchemists believed that an occult chemical transformation of water to stone was possible, and similar fables and humbug were still believed in during the last century.

An exception of this rule was Becher, who taught that crystals could not be formed of ice, as they are found also in localities where neither severe nor long-lasting cold reigns.

Le Roy, in the year 1767, tried to demonstrate before the Academy of Paris, that all experiments made until then did not prove the possibility of changing water into earth. He meant, earth was mixed to the water in a suspended form; that it was not formed anew by each and every distillation, but that only a part of the suspended earth was precipitated, while the greater part of it was distilled over; that by continuous distillation it would be possible to precipitate more and more of the suspended earth, but that the same result could not be obtained with the entire quantity.

It was Lavoisier who proved the true origin of this much-disputed earth; the report of his experiments in this direction is contained in the annals of the Academy of Paris for the year 1770. He showed beyond any doubt, that water, even after long boiling in glass vessels, was not transformed into earth, but that the earth which was found therein after boiling owed its existence to the glass vessel.

The opinion that water was an element was maintained to the close of the eighteenth century.

Cavendish first, in the year 1781, saw that water was produced when hydrogen was burned in the flame of oxygen. In 1783 Watt expressed the opinion that water consisted of oxygen and phlogiston, by which name he very likely meant hydrogen. The undoubted proof for the water's composition of oxygen and hydrogen was given by the great Lavoisier in the same year; the quantitative analysis was first determined by Gay-Lussac, and Humboldt in the year 1805. By numerous exact experiments it is shown that water contains one volume of oxygen and two volumes of hydrogen, or, to express the same fact in weight, it consists of eight parts of oxygen and one part of hydrogen.

Mineral Waters.

ALTHOUGH the first experiments for imitating natural mineral waters may be traced back to the middle of the sixteenth century, yet nearly three centuries passed by before the manufacture of them left the track of aimless experiments and was based upon correct scientific principles.

The gigantic development of chemistry during the last decades of the eighteenth and the first decades of this century enabled scientific men to prove the elementary compounds of the mineral waters both qualitatively and quantitatively.

To Frederick Adolphus Augustus Struve, M. D., proprietor of the Salomon's drug store in Dresden, Saxony, we are indebted for the introduction of the mineral waters into our pharmacopœia. Aften ten years' restless experiments, he opened his first water pavilions in Dresden and Leipsic in the year 1820, the first one in Berlin in the year 1823, together with Geheimrath Soltmann.

The first pioneer who undertook in this country the manufacture of mineral waters with great success, is, to our knowledge, Mr. Charles H. Schultz, and many others followed his footsteps.

Physiology and Diet.

Physiology and Diet.

WE perceive all the impressions that are caused by our surroundings through the medium of our senses; we enjoy nature and its products by these senses and only by these, each of them being equally valuable.

"It is to be especially noted, first, that each nerve of sense is only capable of performing the function designed for it. The nerve of sight does not enable us to hear, and the nerve of smell only enables us to appreciate odors; second, cultivation of the senses, especially if begun in early life, will develop their usefulness; it is true that such training may be carried to the extent of making them a source of misery. Certain persons are painfully conscious of the slightest discord; others almost instantaneously detect, with a feeling of disgust, the inharmonious blending of tints which, to the average person, is a harmonious one; others, still, are made uncomfortable by an odor which is perceptible to none but themselves.

"Cultivation furnishes the accurate hearing of the educated musician, the keen eyesight of the reliable pilot, engineer, and expert microscopist, and the accurate touch of the blind."

If, now, the senses of sight, touch, and hearing may be trained to the blessing of mankind, why should not the same be done with the senses of taste and smell?

In some men these two senses are of higher sensibility than in others, and we have hardly ever heard that these persons were dissatisfied with their superiority.

"Taste is the sense by which we discover and recognize the flavors of substances. It is made possible through the mucous membrane of the tongue, of the soft palate, and of the back part of the throat, these being, in fact, the organs of taste. Only those substances can be tasted which are dissolved. These, by endosmosis, penetrate the mucous membrane, and reach thus the nerves of taste. Accordingly, dry sugar or salt placed upon the tongue is not tasted till it begins to dissolve."

The finer the comminution of food, the sooner is it dissolved and tasted.

Taste is one of the means by which we distinguish between proper and improper articles of food. But in determining the nature of such articles, it is assisted by the other senses. Undoubtedly much pleasure is lent to the taste of certain substances by their appearance and odor; accordingly, one and the same meal will be higher appreciated when served in fine china, on a well-spread table; a drink will be twice and thrice as palatable if prepared by a fine-looking bartender, in fine cut glasses to delight the sight, and when accompanied by a pleasant remark to charm the ear.

Taste in the human being, and also in some of the lower animals, is more or less influenced by imitation, habit, surroundings, and training. Children fancy certain articles of food and dislike others, because other members of the family do the same. That taste may be developed, especially when assisted by the sense of smell, is seen in expert tea and wine tasters.

Although the sense of smell is in man not so acute as the other senses, and its impressions often need to be confirmed by the others, we would be very wrong to undervalue it. Odors, to be recognized, must be presented in a gaseous form, when they are forcibly drawn up by inspiration into the higher portions of the nasal *fossæ.*

There is no doubt that the sense of smell may be highly developed, especially in conjunction with other senses, or in case these are deficient. It is related that a certain blind and deaf mute was able to recognize, by the sense of smell, any person with whom he had previously come into contact.

Every part of an organism is subject to certain alterations, caused by mechanical or chemical action; it gradually ceases to work when the products of reaction are not eliminated, and the loss of material is not equaled by fresh nutritives. Accordingly, we may say that the natural condition of every organism depends upon digestion and assimilation. How these two functions work we do not intend to demonstrate, as it can easily be found in any treatise on Physiology; only this we may be permitted to say, that the materials brought into and dissolved and changed within the organism are the true ministers of said operations. The digested parts of this supply are absorbed by the blood, and deposited by it where need may be, while those parts worthy to be ejected are carried away by the same medium, and delivered for expulsion to kidneys, lungs, glands, etc.

If necessary, we can aid nutrition artificially, and we may do the same in regard to digestion by adding certain compounds, as digestives and tonics (pepsin, pancreatin, muriatic acid, phosphates, etc.), to our food or cordials, and the selection of these compounds is most highly developed in the art of mixing drinks.

Besides food, man requires a number of substances which affect agreeably the tissue and the nerves; they are, to our opinion, necessary for the welfare of an individual, and mainly consist of spices, alcoholic beverages, coffee, tea, chocolate, tobacco, narcotic extracts of plants, as opium, hasheesh, and certain newly discovered drugs, cocaine, chloral, chloroform, ether, etc. They more or less irritate the nervous system, and thus dispel the feeling of pain, fatigue, etc., for a certain space of time, and increase the ability of resistance as also the working power.

They are perfectly harmless as long as there is full supply of nutritives, and while they are taken reasonably.

Among these substances rank first the alcoholic

beverages. A man in normal condition, and by normal work, requires, per day:

> 3½ oz. of albumen,
> 3 oz. of fat,
> 8 oz. of starch and sugar,
> .8 oz. of salt,
> 80 oz. of water.

From this table we see that the fluids are about five times as great as the solids. If this quantity of liquids is not duly supplied, we suffer from a feeling which we call thirst. Beverages are therefore of the highest hygienic and dietetic importance.

In accordance with the highest medical authorities we divide them into:

1. Refreshing beverages: water, mineral waters, acetous waters.
2. Nutritive beverages: emulsions and decoctions of fruits, plants, grain, oats, milk, beef tea, and chocolate.
3. Aromatic beverages: coffee and tea.
4. Alcoholic beverages: wine, beer, alcohol and all fermented drinks.

To build up a healthy body we know that liquids are very important; but we know also that they are still more important in cases of sickness, fever, and all diseases of the digestive apparatus, when the epithelium is unable to absorb anything but liquids.

A look upon the different recipes in this book shows that these drinks, especially the mixed ones, satisfy all requirements, *i.e.*, they are refreshing, nutritive, aromatic, and alcoholic; consequently they must work upon the body most effectively and pleasingly. This is the reason why William's concoctions are longed for by everybody that can afford it, and why they have obtained so wide a fame and reputation.

Diet.

A PROVERB says: "Milk is the wine of the young and wine is the milk of the aged." An intellectual use of alcohol leads to health and happiness, while its abuse naturally is detrimental; but this book is written for thinking people.

Statistics, as well as personal experience, tell us that people enjoying the use of liquors in a reasonable manner, reach a higher age and enjoy a better health than those that are totally abstinent; still worse off are those who want to make others believe that they drink nothing, but are abusive behind their screens.

All countries and states, where prohibition is not sanctioned by law, are on a higher moral level than those where liquors can be secured only under violation of the law.

In numberless cases of sickness physicians do not hesitate one moment to prescribe to the patient medicines containing alcoholic stimulants—especially when it is required to strengthen the body. Why should be detrimental to the strong, what is useful for the weak—

always provided that the strong be of sound intellect and morality?

The present times, nerve-weakening and exciting as they are, require stimulants; and if people cannot get harmless ones they will seek, and, in most cases, find others, the effect of which is highly detrimental for body and mind.

About
Composition of Drinks
and their
Adulterations.

Composition of Drinks, Etc.

THE foundation of all those fluids that are to be taken into consideration for our purpose is formed by one of the most universal elements on our globe—the water.

It is a *conditio sine qua non* both for building up and preserving the whole organic world. A cell, the most primitive of all living beings, *e. g.*, a bathybius, as well as the most highly developed ones, as we see them in the higher organisms of the vegetable and animal kingdoms, contains water as a fundamental basis. Although there are cells, and groups of them, that may retain vitality for thousands of years, even when in dried-up condition, yet this does not affect the relatively higher developed beings in the least. "*Corpora non agunt nisi fluida*" is an old chemical rule, and, indeed, stoppage of all functions, or even death, would occur as soon as the necessary water should not be supplied.

Water is indispensable for fulfilling the physical and chemical processes, among which ranks highest the process of diffusion, or the Endosmosis and Exosmosis.

We feel the lack of water involuntarily, and call this feeling "thirst." The inclination of satisfying this feeling by drinking water, or water-containing liquids, is forced upon us by nature. Thus, thirst compels us to drink, and is, therefore, one of these instinctive impulses that, because being life-preserving, are physiologically of the greatest importance.

How we ought to drink, and what, has already been treated upon; it is only left to show what we must not drink. This task will be solved as soon as we have demonstrated what beverages are composed of, and how they are eventually adulterated.

Although such a treatise ought to be of a strictly chemical character, it will still be interesting, both to the public in general and to manufacturers especially. Therefore we add here, in short but distinct outlines, a description of the composition of fluids, their chemical characteristics when pure, and their possible adulterations.

Water.

It contains, in 100 parts, 88.8 parts of oxygen and 11.1 parts of hydrogen. We know it in three different aggregates—as vapor, as fluid, and as ice. Being one of the chief means for dissolving the most heterogeneous solid substances, and being capable of mixing itself with most of the liquids, it is never found in nature perfectly pure; nor is this at all desirable, as chemically pure water would taste vapid.

Natural water, *e. g.*, rain-water, contains ingredients that were taken from the atmosphere—as nitrogen, carbonic acid gas, dust, salts, germs of organisms, ammonia, nitric and nitrous acids, peroxide of hydrogen.

These ingredients are partly disposed of again by filtering through rocks and gravelly soil. Spring-water contains substances of the soil; these, varying according to the soil's composition, are useful, and in many cases indispensable for the organisms.

The sparkling of the water indicates the presence of gases, without which it is never refreshing. Boiling will drive out all gases, precipitate the bicarbonate of lime and some of the coagulable matters, and destroy some of the germs of disease. Solids—fixa—as we find in water, are chiefly combinations of calcium, magnesium, alkali metals, aluminium, iron, manganese in form of carbonates, chlorides, sulphates, silicates, etc., and organic particles.

Good and palatable drinking water should contain less than $\frac{1}{1000}$ of these fixa; some of them are better not found at all, and if they are, they should be in the smallest possible proportions. The limit of lime is $\frac{1}{5000}$; too great a percentage of magnesia is harmful. Organic particles should be not more than to require $\frac{3}{10}$ to $\frac{6}{10}\%$ of oxygen for their oxidation, $i.\,e.$, as a maximum $\frac{5}{1000}\%$.

The reasons why waters not answering these requirements are doomed, are: Firstly, it is proven beyond any doubt that the spreading of epidemics is in the closest connection with the composition of water, which, having absorbed germs of disease on one place, deposited them on another; secondly, the presence of too great quantities of organic matter, as also of ammonia, nitric and nitrous acids, shows generally an impurity of the water—this being contaminated by filth from cesspools and other sources.

Water, by various methods, may be rid of much of its injurious matter, although a thorough purification is out of question. Filtering through charcoal or oxide of iron will secure water pure enough for use; nor will it lose much of its taste. For special purposes, *f. i.*, for use in hospitals, it is advisable to boil the water first, to cool it, and to add, artificially, carbonic acid gas.

Spring waters, which have a large, and by the taste easily distinguishable, amount of salts, are used mostly for therapeutical purposes, some of them because being palatable and refreshing also instead of ordinary drinking water. We have to dwell only on the latter ones to which belong those having but a few of solid ingredients and dissolved carbonic acid gas, not under 40 vol. per cent. as *f. i.*, Apollinaris, the waters of Heppingen and Dorotheenauer Spring at Carlsbad, etc.; likewise the waters containing alkalies and alkalic muriatic acids with a certain quantity of natrium bicarbonicum and chloride of natrium, besides freely dissolved carbonic acid gas are frequently used as table waters, as those of Vichy, Giesshuebel, Rodna, Ems, Selters, etc.

The waters are either consumed at the springs or bottled; preparations containing their active ingredients, like the pastilles of Bilin, the Carlsbad Salt, etc., are shipped to all parts of the globe; these preparations must be dissolved according to prescription in a certain volume of water to secure the desired therapeutical effect.

Of higher importance, however, are the artificial mineral waters which, in harmony with the exact analysis of the natural waters, are prepared by saturating a solution of the corresponding salts under higher pressure with carbonic acid gas.

With these waters the greater or lesser amount of carbonic acid gas, the greater or lesser purity of the materials used for them, the greater or lesser safety in the emballage are utterly essential; therefore it should be borne in mind where to get these waters from; moreover, waters of certain compositions and established names, such as Vichy, etc., should be prepared under the supervision of expert chemists, and never be ordered from firms that stand under the control of quacks.

Milk.

MILK is composed mainly of water, casein, lactose, fats and mineral ingredients. The fat is only suspended in it, *i.e.*, it is found in infinitely small globules, which float in the colorless solution of the sugar of milk and the protein corpuscles, and which make the fluid appear white.

COMPOSITION OF DRINKS, ETC.

The average composition of good, pure cows' milk should be as follows:

Casein,	5.40 parts
Butter,	4.16 "
Sugar of milk,	4.20 "
Mineral ingredients,	0.54 "
Water,	85.70 "
	100.00

Another composition is given by Dalton:

Water,	87.02 parts
Casein,	4.48 "
Butter,	3.13 "
Sugar of milk,	4.77 "
Mineral ingredients,	0.60 "
	100.00

The mineral ingredients are chiefly kalium, phosphate of calcium, chloride of kalium, and chloride of sodium.

Milk is one of the healthiest, most nutritive and very digestive beverages, and is prescribed very frequently in cases of diseases of the stomach, of phthisis, etc. In cases of poisoning it serves to coat over the irritated mucous membrane, and thus protect it; it works even as an antidote to metallic poisons by precipitating the metals.

It is justly considered the "model food;" necessary as good milk is, it is a common experience to receive it deprived of its cream, diluted with water, or otherwise adulterated by dishonest dealers. A surplus of water renders the milk thin, and gives it a bluish color, which is often covered by yellow dyestuffs. For preserving, salicylic acid, borax, soda, etc., are added; to give diluted milk more body, different ingredients are dissolved in it, as corn-starch, flour, dextrine, glue and emulsions of hemp, poppy, etc. It is capable of absorbing noxious odors and emanations, and may convey the infection of scarlet and typhoid fevers from infected milk-rooms. Great care, therefore, is to be observed in keeping milk. The store-rooms, as the vessels containing it, should be clean and free from odors.

The appearance of milk, its taste, its change in boiling, and after long standing are, for the majority, the only proofs of its quality. The different lactometers and galactometers furnish satisfactory results only in the hands of experts.

Wine.

WHETHER it should be allowed to artificially improve wines, and whether such improvement is to be called adulteration depends entirely on our definition of the word "wine." Wine is either fermented grape-juice, or it is a delicious beverage obtained from fermented grape-juice. These two definitions differ very widely. The first one forbids absolutely the application of any means that might alter the wine, of any substance that is not grown with the grape; according to it wine must neither be blended nor purified, as the very smallest quantities of any stuff used for such a purpose that would and will remain with the wine alters the same, while alcohol, added for blending, originates from the potato and not from the grape-fruit. This definition, to our opinion, is perfectly absurd; the acceptance of it would entitle any judge to condemn any wine-dealer for adulteration as soon as legal proceedings were instituted against him.

The main weight is to be laid on wine being a delicious beverage from grape-juice. It may not always be obtained from simple fermentation of grape-juice; there is many a year when the warming sunrays fail to ripen the fruit of the vine, when the must is sour, and the wine, therefore, turns vapid and pungent, so as to create sadness and grief instead of gladness and joy, when taken by us poor mortals.

Depriving such must of its surplus of acids, and enhancing its percentage of sugar means to produce a wine agreeable to the palate, and not injurious to the health, while the taste of the natural wine would have filled every one with disgust.

Adulteration of any article may only be spoken of in case the value of said article be diminished, or substances be added that are likely to injure the health.

In improving wine the following methods are mainly adopted, and named after their inventors:

1. Chaptalizing: The surplus of acids in wine is neu-

tralized, and the deficient sugar is added. Carbonate of calcium is used for neutralizing, in the proportion of 100 parts of chalk to 150 parts of acids. To add the missing sugar we first determine by a saccharometer what percentage of sugar is contained in the wine. Let this be 15%, then we will increase the sugar from 20-24%.

2. Gallizing: Gall has, immediately after the picking, the ripe berries separated from the less ripe ones. The first ones are worked with alone. From the unripe ones he obtains a juice which he does not neutralize, but which he dilutes with water until a certain degree of acid is reached, when he corrects also the lack of sugar.

Beyse states of gallized wines: 1. A constantly good wine may be obtained, even in poor years. 2. They stand transportation without change. 3. They require only a year's attention and care. 4. They contain more alcohol. 5. The quantity is increased, while the quality is improved.

Of other methods we only name that of Pétiot.

Wines are, especially right after fermentation, liable to many changes which alter them for the worse, or may even utterly ruin them. Pasteur, the eminent French chemist, has taught us the nature of these diseases, which are due to the presence of bacilli or germs.

As general hints for protection are to be minded:

Try to stop the development of these germs by the most careful cleanliness of all vessels and rooms by utmost scouring and extensive ventilating. Infected vessels, barrels, tubs, etc., are to be removed from the cellars, and, be this impossible, the disinfection must be done there.

The percentage of alcohol, as far as it is not due to blending, is in closest connection with the quantity of sugar in the must; no wine can contain more than seventeen vol. per cent. of alcohol, as with this degree the transformation of sugar into alcohol by fermentation is stopped, and any surplus is caused by blending. All southern wine-growers are fond of increasing the sugar in their wines, thus, Australia produces hardly any wine below 26%.

The coloring of wines offers many chances for adulteration. Immense quantities of white wines are thus made red wines, and even liquids that can boast of no relationship to the grape-juice at all are transformed into red wines by coloring materials.

Dyestuffs mainly used for this purpose are: berries from *sambucus niger*, *sambucus ebulus*, *vaccinium myrtillus*, *ligustrum vulgaris*, *phytolacca decandra*, the flowers of *malva arborea*, *althea rosea*, and *malva silvestris*, beets, logwood and Brazilwood, cochineal, indigo, fuchsine, and other aniline colors.

Of these dyestuffs the aniline colors are easiest to detect, while natural colors, having very great similarity to the natural dyestuff of wine, sometimes render it, even to an expert, difficult to prove their presence.

Beer.

BEER—or to call it by the name that is at present more *en vogue*, Lager—consists, or at least ought to consist, of a fermented extract of malt and hops. While in the first quarter of this century this healthy and agreeable beverage used to be prepared often enough from a mixture containing many violent poisons, as Indian hemp, opium, sulphuric acid, sulphate of iron, etc.—nay, the addition of strychnia, even, was suspected—the principal adulterations of it, at the present time, consist of water, to increase the bulk of the fluid, and burnt sugar and salt, to restore in a measure its color and flavor. The addition of water does not render beer injurious, but it cheats people out of their money. Burnt sugar, or treacle, was extensively employed, with the view of increasing the dark color of porter, stout, or other heavy beers; the ingredient known as *essentia bina*, formerly used in the manufacture of beer, consisted of moist sugar boiled in an iron vessel until it had become syrupy, perfectly black, and extremely bitter.

The acidity in beer is very desirable; it depends, probably, on the presence of malic and lactic acid. In many cases, however, acetic acid, or vinegar, is formed in beer from a decomposition of excessive fermentation of its sugar; the beverage is then very sour, and unfit for use. There is some reason to believe that sulphuric acid is occasionally used to give astringency to beer, in which case the addition of chloride of barium to the liquor will cause the formation of a bulky precipitate insoluble in nitric acid. Sulphate of iron was, and probably is still, employed for restoring the flavor of beer. Should this chemical be present in an alcoholic beverage, by adding ammonia and sulphide of ammonium to the fluid a black precipitate will be produced.

More recently, trials have been made to substitute picric acid instead of hops; beer prepared in this way is nothing but a solution of glucose, augmented or rather spiced with picric acid. Taste by itself fails in helping us to distinguish the presence of this acid, but Lassaigne gave us the means of detecting even the slightest proportions of said acid in beer. By shaking good, unadulterated beer with an excess of pulverized burned bone-dust it loses all its color, as the powder absorbs all the dyestuffs; but when doing the same with beer adulterated by addition of picric acid, it will not lose its yellowish tint.

It would be a great comfort to all beer-drinkers to know that such adulterations belong to the past; but, though sorry to say so, we are of the opinion of old Dr. Faust: "It's true the message I do hear, yet I cannot believe it."

Spirits.

In hardly any article of merchandise so many adulterations occur as in the stronger alcoholic liquids. And to these falsifications it is due that the use of alcohol so often shows its most detrimental effect on the health, especially on the brain of man.

Spirits may be adulterated with water, sugar, capsicum, cinnamon or cassia, various sulphates, free sulphuric acid and lead. Water has been added to them in such a degree that their commercial value was reduced to the enormous extent of more than one-half. This lack of body was covered partly by sugar. Hassall says in his *Adulterations of Food*, etc.: "It is impossible to conceive of more scandalous adulterations of spirits than those by cayenne pepper or grains of paradise, for they are almost equally hot and pungent. The introduction into the stomach of raw spirits is sufficiently destructive of itself, but the addition of such powerful and acrid substances as cayenne pepper and grains of paradise forms a compound which no human stomach or system, however strong, could long withstand."

The different kinds of spirits are obtained in a comparatively crude state from the grain by the distiller. They are afterward submitted to purification by the rectifier, as well as procured of a higher strength. The impurity of raw spirits arises principally from the presence of a peculiar volatile oil, termed fusel oil, and possessing very deleterious properties. Dr. Taylor remarks of this oil, "that in small quantities it produces intoxication. I have experienced the effects of the vapour and found them to be giddiness, accompanied with a feeling of suffocation and a sense of falling. Headache followed which lasted half an hour." Two drachms of the oil killed a rabbit in two hours, three drachms in an hour, half an ounce in a quarter of an hour, and one ounce in four minutes. Much of the unwholesomeness of spirits imperfectly rectified arises from its contamination with fusel oil.

To show what infernal concoctions are served to the public we put down only one recipe out of a great number, taken from a book that is said to be the best on the market.

To manufacture whiskey, the following Bourbon Oil recipe is given:

Take Fusel Oil,	64 oz.
" Acetate of Potassium,	4 "
" Sulphuric Acid,	4 "
Dissolve Sulphate of Copper,	½ "
and Oxalate of Ammonium,	½ "
each in water,	4 "
Add Black Oxide of Manganese,	1 "

Place them all in a glass percolator and let them rest for twelve hours. Then percolate and put into a glass still, and distill half a gallon of the Bourbon Oil.

Sapienti sat!

Ethnography.

Ethnography.

THE quantity of food required by a normal man depends not only upon his size, the greater amount of muscular work, but, in the first place, on the climate. A body exposed to a cool, bracing atmosphere, or to extreme cold demands an increased supply of food. The ravenous appetite noticed among the inhabitants of cold climates may be due in part to the fact that their food-supply is very irregular, as to make them eat to excess when supplied with food. According to Dr. Hayes, the arctic explorer, the daily ration of the Esquimaux, is from twelve to fifteen pounds of meat, about one-third of which is fat. The demand for fatty substances increases with the greater cold; hence the Esquimaux as all other inhabitants of the arctic regions, do hardly know anything drinkable but fatty beverages, such as cod-liver oil, sperm oil, etc., of which they use from four to five pounds daily.

The temperate zones, varying very much in their temperature and moisture according to the different elevations, the greater or lesser distance from oceans, the greater or lesser exposure to warm and cold winds, require what we might name a general diet. People in the parts nearer to the tropics will regulate their diet in accordance with the rules prescribed for these, while those nearer to the arctic regions will have to accommodate themselves to their demands. Everywhere, however, we find a desire for fermented beverages, be it wine or beer, whiskey or brandy.

The Kirghisians' favorite drink is the Kumyss, prepared from fermented horse-milk.

The inhabitants of Korea (Eastern Asia) prepare their wine of rice or millet, of which they are extremely fond.

The Japanese make their wine mostly of rice, and call it Saki.

Although we must warn every man of the Caucasian race not to yield too much to the enjoyment of alcoholic beverages within the tropics, because there everything ought to be shunned that aids in producing more individual heat and needs much oxygen for combustion, yet we must state that this restriction must be confined to white people only. The indigenous inhabitants do not seem to suffer at all from their fermented beverages, at least not more than white people from theirs. Ample proofs of it we find in the publications of explorers. In the following we want to give some testimonials for the correctness of our assertion:

"As the people were amiable .... we had soon an abundance of .... plantain and palm wines for cheer." —STANLEY: *Through the Dark Continent*, October 18, 1876.

"Tippu Tib gave a banquet of rice and roasted sheep to the expedition; and malofu, or palm wine, from Mpsika Island, assisted to maintain the high spirits."—*Ibid*, December 26, 1876.

"We supposed them to be dancing and enjoying their palm wine, the delicious and much-esteemed malofu."—*Ibid*, February 10, 1877.

"But the people, upon whom our liberality had produced too strong an effect, would not permit us to do so (leave) until we had further celebrated our acquaintance with copious draughts of their delicious wine (sweet maramba or banana wine)."—*Ibid*, March 26, 1875.

"With rather glazed eyes they offered us some of the equatorial nectar. The voyage had been long on this day, and we were tired, and it might be that we sighed for such cordial, refreshing drink as was now proffered to us. At any rate, we accepted their hospitable gift, and sucked heartily, with bland approval of the delicacy of the liquid."—*Ibid*, April, 1875.

"Refreshments were not wanting to cheer the dancers. Great masses of beef were roasted over glorious fires, and many jars of beer and maramba, brought from Bwina and Komeh, invited the special attention of the thirsty."—*Ibid*, July 17, 1875.

"A great drinking of maramba wine and potent beer followed."—*Ibid*, October 29, 1875.

The Barabra in northeast Africa prepare a beverage, "Merissa," of the flour of Duchn, by pouring over it boiling water and letting it ferment for awhile. The yellowish-looking, sparkling, sour-tasting fluid is changed to a beer by adding some herbs. The Barabras are ever so fond of this liquid.

The Ketchuas, the descendants of the old Incas, know no higher enjoyment than drunkenness; each festival is celebrated by excessive drinking. Their favorite beverage is "Chicha" (pronounced Tschitscha), a fermented maize decoction, cooling, opening, nutritious, and intoxicating, if taken in great quantities.

The Indians of the Caribbean Sea prepare fermented beverages from the Mandioca root. Paiwari, Paiwa, Kassiri, are the names of just as many fermented drinks.

A specific beverage of the Hottentots is the "Krii," or honey-beer; it is made of wild honey, water and the fermented decoction of the Krii-root. Likewise they understand how to prepare alcoholic liquids by infusing berries.

Between the Senegal and the Niger everything is concentrated upon the enjoyment of alcoholic drinks. The negro—fond of drinks, may it be wine, beer, or alcohol—is willing to acknowledge the supremacy of the European, and is an enemy to Mohammedanism. *Vice versa*, the negro that does not drink is a follower of Mohammed, whether he knows who Mohammed was or not. It may occur that a drinker, after a bacchanal, in repentance of it, shaves his hair closely, with the exception of the centre; then he is "Tub," or a convert, and will join the public religious services of the Mohammedans. The drinker, however, wears his full hair. If he be obliged to require the services of a barber, *i. e.*, of a piece of glass or a sharpened shell, he will take great care to leave a wreath of hair, in order never to be taken for a "Tub." From afar you may distinguish with comparative surety the one that does not drink (Sering) from the one that drinks (Tjedo), respectively, the Mohammedan from the heathen or Christian. Both hate and despise each other, and some tribes, as the Diobas and the Sarrars, shoot every Mohammedan at sight. On the other side, ask a believer in Islamism what should be done with a drinker, and he will make a significant motion with his hand around the throat, and in most cases a drinker is beheaded on the spot. But as the proverb says, "*Il y a des accommodements avec le ciel*," the teetotalers help themselves by swallowing rather large quantities of cologne-water.

# Our Ancestors.

Description of a Greek Banquet.

Before the invited guest went to the entertainment he made his toilette: that is, he bathed, perfumed himself, and donned his best clothes and shoes.

The table was usually spread in the *andronitis*, or reception room for men, and the guest, after exchanging salutations with his entertainers, took the place assigned to him, the most honorable being that at the side of the host. Servants removed the shoes of the guests and purified the feet from the dust of the streets. Then they reclined upon couches with bright coverings and hangings, resting the left arm upon a cushion, so as to leave the right hand free. As a rule, there were two guests to each couch. Before each the slaves placed a table spread with viands, and brought meat, fish, and sauces in dishes, and bread, cakes, and fruit in baskets. The guest had no plate nor knife for himself, and as for forks, they were unknown, but a spoon was placed at his disposal. The meat was served cut into small pieces, which he took with the fingers of the right hand, and dipped into the sauces. After the meal, as before it, the servants carried around water to wash the hands, and during the meal the fingers were wiped, if necessary, on bread or a piece of dough placed for the purpose.

The repast usually consisted of two courses, of which

the first was fish and meat, with the vegetables and other *hors-d'œuvres*, and the second the dessert of pastry, cakes, and fruit.

While the meal proper continued, there was no drinking, nor was it the custom to converse while eating. Conversation began with the second part of the entertainment, the symposion or carousal, for which the tables were removed, and the floor cleansed of all fragments. Other tables were then brought in by the servants, covered with salted cakes—a kind of bretzels—cheese and other viands provocative of thirst.

The great mixing bowls were brought in, also pitchers of water cooled in snow, and jugs of unmixed wines, ladle-shaped dippers, beakers, and cups deep and shallow, of graceful forms, and the queer horn-shaped vessels, called rhyta. The youngest and handsomest slaves were chosen to wait on the guests, who crowned their heads and garlanded their breasts with myrtle and violets, ivy and roses, not merely as a sign of festivity, but to cool their glowing temples, and, as they thought, to counteract the heady qualities of the wine. Music was then brought in, song and dance delighted ear and eye, and Bacchos, attended by the Muses and the Graces, ruled the hour, often until all were sunk in intoxication.

The Greek loved wine, and honored it in art and song. He loved it not merely as a means of sensual enjoyment: he used it as the care-dispeller, the bringer of joy and mirth. Wine raised the spirits of the youth, and taught age to forget its gray hairs and disregard its infirmities.

Description of a Roman Banquet.

The chief meal of the Romans took place in the evening, and was the last meal of the day.

In early morning, before going out, it was the custom to break the fast on bread and salt, eaten with fruit, cheese or olives; about noon followed the luncheon, or prandium; and then about midway between noon and sunset, though often much later, the cœna, which might be prolonged far into the night. The prandium was sometimes more substantial, and comprised fish, eggs, shell-fish and wine; but the proper art of the kitchen was reserved for the cœna. This consisted usually of a variety of entrées, provocative of appetite, followed by two very substantial courses and a dessert.

But the Romans were not at first thus luxurious. In the early time a kind of porridge of pulse formed their principal food, and this, with the addition of vegetables and leguminous fruits, especially beans, remained the diet of the lower classes at all times. Down to the year 174 B. C., there were neither cooks nor bakers in the city who regularly followed their trades.

The Asiatic wars first made the Romans acquainted

with the luxuries of the table, and furnished them with cooks, bakers and confectioners in the persons of slaves who were sold at high prices. Thenceforth gastronomy became a study, and the ordering and preparation of a dinner a science and an art. The Republic had already had a Lucullus, whose name ever after was associated with sumptuous repasts; but the gastronomic art, for which he was so renowned, did not attain its perfection and glory until imperial times. Then, when Rome had extended her sway over the whole world, the expansion of trade and intercourse brought the dainties of all lands to the capital; the farthest East, and the farthest West, the delicacies of India, the spices of Arabia, the fish and shell-fish of the Atlantic, the game of Gaul and Germany, and the dates of the oases, all met in the Roman kitchen. The Emperor Vitellius, perhaps the most enormous eater that the Empire ever knew, sent out his legions to hunt game where it was found in the highest perfection, and employed his fleets in furnishing his table with fresh fish. So many arms were set in motion by a single stomach! At this time it was that all the breeding and fattening establishments were erected. Remarkably large or fine fish were bought by wealthy gourmands at fabulous prices, as many anecdotes tell us, but probably more for the sake of notoriety than anything else.

Fish, oysters, snails, mussels and other shell-fish, of which the Roman kitchen boasted a greater variety

DESCRIPTION OF A ROMAN BANQUET.

than our own, were supplied from all parts of the Empire, and the epicures knew well where the choicest were to be found, and the most delicate modes of preparing them. The mullet or sea-barbel, a fish highly esteemed, was often brought alive to the table that the guests might have visible proof of its freshness. When the favorite Italian oysters began to pall on the appetite, recourse was had to the "natives" of Britain.

The villa furnished fowls, which were fattened in the dark, and ducks and geese fed with figs and dates; the *volarium* or aviary: fieldfares, snipes, quails, pheasants, and smaller birds.

Storks, cranes, flamingos, and especially peacocks, were also often served at Roman tables. Vitellius and Apicius—that gourmand who devoured his whole large fortune and, when reduced to his last million, killed himself because life was no longer worth having—prepared a dish of the tongues of flamingoes, and Elagabalus of their brains. Among quadrupeds the pig was in highest favor, and more than fifty ways were known of dressing its flesh.

Wild boars were often served whole, and epicures could tell by the flavor from what region the animal came. Sausages of various kinds were a favorite dish, both hot and cold; and hucksters on the streets served them to customers from small, portable stoves. The best sausages, as well as the best hams, came from Gaul. There was an abundant supply of salads and vegetables; asparagus was cultivated to a large size; many kinds of cabbages were grown, with turnips, artichokes, pumpkins and cucumbers, peas and beans, mushrooms and truffles, and many plants and herbs used for flavoring.

Nor did the Roman table lack rare and choice wines, kept in jars or bottles of baked clay. They were prized in proportion to their age; and each jar bore a label, showing in whose consulship the wine had been made. Campania furnished the best Italian wines, of which the Caecuban held the first rank, the Falernian the next, while the third place was claimed by several vintages; but whoever was forced to drink the Vatican was an object of general commiseration. Greek wines, too, had their place in the Roman cellars. As, with the increasing luxury the customs at the table were more and more fashioned after those of the Greeks, though incomparably more luxurious, so, like the Greek, the Roman rarely drank wine undiluted. He mingled it with water, and cooled it with snow; while for the winter he had a warm drink—the *calda*, made of wine, water, honey, and spice, for preparing which there was a special vessel, the *caldarium*, with a small furnace of charcoal in the interior, on the principle of the Russian samovar.

Still another beverage, called *mulsum*, which was drunk at breakfast, was prepared of must, honey, and spices.

The Roman table was thus liberally provided, and though many dishes seem to us of questionable taste, still, the achievements of Romans in the culinary line do them high credit. Even in Cæsar's time, at a pontifical banquet, attended by six priests and as many priestesses, the following was the menu: First course (intended merely as a whet to appetite): conger eels, oysters, two kinds of mussels, thrushes on asparagus, fat fowls, a ragout of oysters and other shell-fish, with black and white *marrons*. Second course: a variety of shell-fish and other marine animals, becaficos, haunches of venison, a wild boar, a pasty of becaficos and other birds. Third and principal course: the udders of swine, boar's head, fricassee of fish, fricassee of sow's udder, ducks of various kinds, hares, roast fowls with pastry, and Picentine bread.

This by no means meagre bill of fare was far surpassed in later times, especially in the pastry and confectionery; and this part of the repast was distinguished by the originality and artistic forms of its devices, in which the confectioner rivaled the statuary.

A Roman Banquet Described

BY

QUINTUS HORATIUS FLACCUS.

SATIRARUM LIBER II. VIII. TRANSL. BY P. FRANCIS.

[This is obviously a satire on a person of bad taste giving a dinner to men of superior rank, where every delicacy of the season, though commended with ostentation by the host, is either tainted by being kept too long, or spoiled by bad cookery, and disgraced by the awkwardness of the attendants.]

HORACE, FUNDANIUS

HORACE.

They told me that you spent the jovial night
With Nasidienus, that same happy wight,
From early day, or you had been my guest;
But, prithee, tell me how you liked the feast.

FUNDANIUS.

Sure never better.

HORACE.

    Tell me, if you please,
How did you first your appetite appease?

FUNDANIUS.

First, a Lucanian boar, of tender kind,
Caught, says our host, in a soft southern wind:
Around him lay whatever could excite,
With pungent force, the jaded appetite;
Rapes, lettuce, radishes, anchovy brine,
With skerrets and the lees of Coan wine.
This dish removed, a slave, expert and able,
With purple napkin wiped a maple table;

Another sweeps the fragments of the feast,
That nothing useless might offend the guest.
Like Ceres' priestess dark Hydaspes rears
A bowl that Cæcuba's rich vintage bears,
While of the Chian grape, the much-famed juice,
But dead and vapid, Alcon's hand produce.
"If Alban or Falernian please you more,"
So says our host, "you may have both, good store."
Poor wealth, indeed!

HORACE.

But, tell me, who were there,
Thus happy, to enjoy such luscious fare?

FUNDANIUS.

On the first couch I haply lay between
Viscus and Varius, if aright I ween;
Servilius and Vibidius both were there,
Brought by Mæcenas; and with him they share
The middle bed. Our master of the feast
On the third couch, in seat of honor placed,
Porcius betwixt and Nomentanus lies—
Porcius, who archly swallows custard pies—
While Nomentanus, with his finger, shows
Each hidden dainty, which so well he knows;
For we, poor folk, unknowing of our feast,
Eat fish and wild fowl—of no common taste.
But he, to prove how luscious was the treat,
With a broiled flounder's entrails crowds my plate.
Then told me: Apples are more ruddy bright,
If gathered by fair Luna's waning light.
He best can tell you where the difference lies—
But here Servilius to Vibidius cries:
"Sure to be poison'd, unrevenged we die,
Unless we drink the wretched talker dry.
Slave, give us larger glasses!" Struck with dread,
A fearful pale our landlord's face o'erspread;

Great were his terrors of such drinking folk,
Because with too much bitterness they joke.
Or that hot wines, dishonoring his feast,
Deafen the subtle judgment of the taste.
    When our two champions had their goblets crown'd,
We did them justice, and the glass went round;
His parasites alone his anger fear'd,
And the full flask unwillingly they spar'd.
In a large dish an outstretch'd lamprey lies,
With shrimps all floating round; the master cries:
"This fish, Mæcenas, full of roe was caught,
For, after spawning time, its flesh is naught.
The sauce is mixed with olive-oil; the best
And purest from the vats Venafran press'd.
And as it boil'd we pour'd in Spanish brine,
Nor less than five year old Italian wine.
A little Chian's better when 'tis boil'd,
By any other it is often spoil'd.
Then was white pepper o'er it gently pour'd,
And vinegar of Lesbian vintage sour'd.
I, first among the men of sapience, knew,
Roquets and herbs in cockle brine to stew;
Though in the same rich pickle, 'tis confess'd,
His unwash'd crayfish sage Curtillus dress'd."

*   *   * . *   *   *   *   *

But lo ! the canopy that o'er us spreads,
Tumbled in hideous ruin on our heads;
With dust, how black ! not such the clouds arise
When o'er the plain a northern tempest flies.
Some horrors yet more horrible we dread,
But raise us when we found the danger fled.

*   *   *   *   *   *   *   *

Poor Rufus droop'd his head, and sadly cried,
As if his only son untimely died.
Sure he had wept, till weeping ne'er had end,
But Nomentanus thus upraised his friend:
"Fortune, thou cruelest of powers divine,
To joke poor mortals is a joke of thine."

While Varius, with a napkin, scarce suppress'd
His laughter.   Balatro, who loves a jest,
Cries: "Such is the lot of life, nor must you claim
For all your toils a fair return of fame.
While you are tortured thus, and torn with pain,
A guest like me, polite to entertain,
With bread well baked, with sauces season'd right,
With slaves in waiting, elegantly tight,
Down rush the canopies, a trick of fate,
Or a groom footman, stumbling, breaks a plate.
Good fortune hides, adversity calls forth
A landlord's genius and a leader's worth."
  To this mine host: "Thou ever gentle guest,
May all thy wishes by the gods be bless'd,
Thou best good man!" But when we saw him rise,
From bed to bed the spreading whisper flies.
No play was half so fine.

Horace.

But prithee say,
How afterwards you laugh'd the time away.

Fundanius.

"Slaves (cries Vibidius), have you broach'd the cask?
How often must I call for the other flask?"
With some pretended joke our laugh was dress'd,
Servilius ever seconding the jest;
When you, great host, return'd with alter'd face,
As if to mend with art your late disgrace.
  The slaves behind, in mighty charger bore
A crane, in pieces torn, and powder'd o'er
With salt and flour, and a white gander's liver
Stuff'd fat with figs, bespoke the curious giver,
Besides the wings of hares, for, so it seems,
No man of luxury the back esteems.
  Then saw we blackbirds, with o'erroasted breast,
Laid on a board, and ring-doves rumpless dress'd!

> Delicious fare ! did not our host explain
> Their various qualities in endless strain,
> Their various natures; but we fled the feast,
> Resolved in vengeance nothing more to taste;
> As if Canidia, with empoison'd breath,
> Worse than a serpent's, blasted it with death.

A Royal Feast Among the Huns.

A. D. 448.

(Edward Gibbon: *The Decline and Fall of the Roman Empire*.)

The Roman ambassadors, both of the East and of the West, were twice invited to the banquets where Attila feasted with the princes and nobles of Scythia. Maximin and his colleagues were stopped on the threshold, till they had made a devout libation to the health and prosperity of the king of the Huns, and were conducted, after this ceremony, to their respective seats in a spacious hall. The royal table and couch, covered with carpets and fine linen, was raised by several steps in the midst of the hall; and a son, an uncle, or, perhaps, a favorite king were admitted to share the simple and homely repast of Attila. Two lines of small tables, each of which contained three or four guests, were ranged in order on either hand, the right was esteemed the most honorable; but the Romans ingenuously confess they were placed on the left, and that Beric, an unknown chieftain, most probably of the Gothic race, preceded the representatives of Theodosius and Valentinian.

The barbarian monarch received from his cupbearer a goblet filled with wine, and courteously drank to the health of the most distinguished guest, who rose from his seat, and expressed in the same manner his loyal and respectful vows. This ceremony was successively performed for all, or at least for the illustrious persons, of the assembly; and a considerable time must have been consumed, since it was thrice repeated as each course or service was placed on the table. But the wine still remained after the meat had been removed, and the Huns continued to indulge their intemperance long after the sober and decent ambassadors of the two empires had withdrawn themselves from the nocturnal banquet. Yet before they retired they enjoyed a singular opportunity of observing the manners of the nation in their convivial amusements. Two Scythians stood before the couch of Attila and recited verses, which they had composed to celebrate his valor and his victories. A profound silence prevailed in the hall, and the attention of the guests was captivated by the vocal harmony, which revived and perpetuated the memory of their own exploits: a martial ardor flashed from the eyes of the warriors, who were impatient for battle; and the tears of the old men expressed their generous despair that they could no longer partake the danger and glory of the field. This entertainment, which might be considered as a school of military virtue, was succeeded by a farce that debased the dignity of human nature. A Moorish and a Scythian buffoon (dwarf) successively excited the mirth of the rude spectators by their deformed figure, ridiculous dress, antic gestures, absurd speeches, and the strange, unintelligible confusion of the Latin, the Gothic, and the Hunnic languages; and the hall resounded with loud and licentious peals of laughter. In the midst of this intemperate riot, Attila alone, without a change of countenance, maintained his steadfast and inflexible gravity, which was never relaxed, except on the entrance of Irnac, the youngest of his sons: he embraced the boy with a smile of paternal tenderness, gently pinched him on the cheek, and betrayed a partial affection, which was justified by the assurance of his prophets that Irnac would be the future support of his family and empire.

A Menu of Emperor Charles V. (1519–1556).

[This is a dinner bill of fare, with which the city of Halle honored Charles V. on a fast-day.]

1. Raisins in malt-flour,
2. Fried eggs,
3. Pancakes,
4. Steamed carrots,
5. Fried slices of bread,
6. A covered porridge,
7. A high pasty,
8. Pea-soup with marrow, covered richly with peas and eggs,
9. Yellow codfish, boiled in butter,
10. Carps, boiled,
11. Fried fish, with bitter oranges, spiced,
12. Sweet pikes,
13. Pulverized kernels, with almonds,
14. Maize in almonds' milk,
15. Fried fish, with small olives,
16. Cakes,
17. Pears and confect.

"His Majesty ate heartily, God bless His appetite, and took only three draughts from a Venetian glass."

What Kinds of Wines
And in Which Order
Should They be Served at a Repast?

What Kinds of Wines and in Which Order Should They be Served at a Repast?

WINE is, at each and every festival, of such importance, that it at least requires the same care and attention as the meals: if these form but the material part of a banquet, then wine represents its intellectual, psychical contents, and there is nothing more provoking to a true gourmand than to have the most select meals served with ordinary or inferior wines, or in improper combination. It requires much knowledge and intellect, not only to select really good and genuine wines, and to keep them in the best possible condition, but to pick them out deliberately in harmony with the dishes, and to have them brought on the table in a manner to show all their excellency. The old Greeks and Romans used to mix their wines with water, and this habit was followed through the greater part of the mediæval age, because adulteration of wines was nearly unknown. The praiseworthiness of certain brands was found out but gradually, and several interesting little stories may illustrate this: A butler of Bishop John de Fugger had to travel ahead of His Eminence and to mark every inn where he should find good and palatable wine, with the word *Est* (is). Now, one day he came to Monte Fiasco, and was so delighted with the beverage he found there, that he marked on the entrance door of the inn: "*Est, Est, Est.*" The bishop came, remained there, and drank himself to a blessed death.

Less known, but not less interesting, is the following story which, however, seems to be in little accordance with the historical facts we put down in regard to champagne wines. Emperor Wenzel (1378-1400) came to Rheims in the year 1397 to make a treaty with Charles VI. of France. He found the wine that grew in the vicinity superior to all others; on its account he delayed the treaty, and when, finally, it was agreed upon he could not yet possibly make up his mind to leave the so hospitable city of Rheims, but devoted another entire year to the study of the wines of the neighborhood.

Besides the discrimination of wines, according to their color, into red and white ones, we may divide them also as follows: 1. Sweet, or so-called liquor wines. 2. Acidulous wines. 3. Tannic wines. 4. Alcoholic wines. 5. Sparkling wines.

We do not intend to bore the kind reader by enumerating the hundreds of brands both in this country and in Europe; we want only to show how, at a dinner, wines should be combined with the different courses. For every two to four guests a bottle of red wine and one of a light white wine is required, *e.g.*, St. Julien, Pontet Canet, or Ober-Ingelheimer, Affenthaler and Markgräfler; after the soup, port wine, Madeira, sherry, Malvasy, Marsala, etc.; selected wines are served in small glasses. A good white wine, as Forster, Rauenthaler, Pisporter, or another Rhine or Moselle wine, but light, is given with the fish; with the relevés and entrées, Bordeaux; with ragouts, mayonnaises, or vegetables and chops, Burgundy or heavy Rhine wine; with the roast, champagne; to pasties and entremets serve a fine, red wine, but not too acidulous, *e. g.*, St. Emilion, Brane Mouton, Château Margaux; for the dessert, a heavy sweet wine, as Malaga, Muscat-Lunel, Alicante, Rivesaltes, Tokay, Ménescher, Frontignan, Syracuse, or Greek wine.

This is, of course, only to be followed at great banquets when you want to make a display; for smaller parties a good Bordeaux, a good Rhine wine or Moselle, and perhaps a bottle of champagne, or one of sweet wine will be sufficient.

For *"déjeuners"* mostly a light red and a white wine are served, with one or two brands of heavy sweet wines. If the *déjeuner* be warm, you give Chablis to oysters, Moselle to fish or meat salads, Bordeaux to chops, roast beef, etc., white Burgundy or fine Rhine wine to roasts; to bread, butter, and cheese English ale, Bavarian beer or porter, or, at discretion, a Spanish or Hungarian wine.

For supper never serve any of those heavy sweet

wines, but take Bordeaux, Rhine wine, or another good white wine, and let follow champagne or a bowl.

All these wines must have a certain degree of temperature when they develop their virtues best; without it the "bouquet" of a wine will never be developed fully. The lighter white wines must be served very fresh and cool; put inferior Rhine wines and Moselle on ice, but fine Rhine wines and white Bordeaux must never be too cold; red wine ought to have a temperature of about 58°–60° F.; Burgundy is to be of the common cellar temperature, as also Hungarian wines, Madeira, Malaga, and all heavy sweet wines; the latter ones ought to be rather warm than cold, and be taken from the cellar a while before using. Champagne, however, must be very cold and be *frappé* for this purpose, *i. e.*, it must be placed in a cooler with cracked ice mixed with a little salt.

Some Sample Menus.

◁ FESTAL DINNER ▷

IN HONOR OF THE PRESENCE OF
HIS IMPERIAL ROYAL HIGHNESS, THE CROWN-PRINCE

FREDERICK WILLIAM,
–IN–
HAMBOURG, APRIL 20, 1877.

Real Turtle Consommé.	Moët et Chandon, Grand Crémant Impérial, Rœderer carte blanche.
Truffes de Perigord en serviette Timbales à la Richelieu.	1834 Sherry.
Turbot, Sauce Hollandaise, Saumon du Rhin, Sauce Genevoise.	1868 Rauenthalerberg-Auslese, 1868 Königsmosel.
Filet de Bœuf à la Jardinière.	1858 Château-Leoville Poyféré.
Poulardes du Mans Truffées.	1858 Clos-Vougeot.
Escalopes de Foie Gras à la Parisienne.	1858 Hermitage Rouge.
Bastion de Homards au Naturel.	1811 Vin de Madère.
Fonds d'Artichauts à l'Italienne, Asperges en Branches.	1858 Clos-Montrachet.
Bécasses en Canapés aux Laitues.	1859 Pichon Longueville.
Gelée de vin du Champagne, Nougat Blanc à la Turque, Crême d'Ananas.	1864 Château d'Yquem Crême de Tête.
Beurre et Fromage.	1831 Vin d'Oporto, rouge et blanc.
Desserts et Fruits.	1864 Château Lafitte, Original Schlossabzug.

SCHLOSS HOTEL, HEIDELBERG.

Festal Dinner of the Secretaries of the Treasuries

OF GERMANY,

August 5, 1878.

Mock-turtle Soup, Chicken Soup.	*Sherry,* *Madeira.*
Trout, with Butter and Potatoes, Turbot, Sauce Hollandaise.	*Rhinegold.*
Venison, with Mushrooms, Tenderloin, with Sauce à l'Empereur.	*Markgräfler,* *Affenthaler.*
Sweetbread, with Truffles, Lobsters, with Sauce à la Tartare.	*Liebfrauenmilk,* *St. Julien.*
New Sauerkraut, with Partridges. Ham, boiled in Burgundy.	*Weihenstephan Beer.*
Artichokes, with smoked Salmon.	*Johannisberger Cabinet,* *Château Larose.*
French Poultry, Salad, and different preserved Fruits.	*Louis Rœderer,* *carte blanche.*

Plum Pudding, with Vanilla Sauce,
Maraschino Gelée, with preserved Fruits.
Ice-cream.
Fruits.
Dessert.

COLOGNE, SEPTEMBER 28, 1878.

UNVEILING OF THE ROYAL MONUMENT.

GUERZENICH-BANQUET.

Salad of Crawfish.	Old Sherry.
Chicken Soup, Mock-turtle Soup.	1870 Pisporter.
Fine Ragout in shells, Turbot, with Mushrooms.	1874 Solberg, Marquis de Therme.
Ham in Madeira, Sauerkraut, with Partridges, Green Peas, with Salmon and Tongue, Sweetbread-Fricassée, with Morels à la Bruxelles.	1874 Erdener Treppchen Auslese, 1874 Walporzheimer Domlay, 1865 Grand Vin Château Margaux.
Venison, with canned Fruits, French Capons, with Salad, Lobsters, Strasbourg Goose-liver Pastry.	1868 Schloss Vollradser, 1868 Steinberger Cabinet, 1862 Johannisberger.
Ice-cream, Cakes, French Grapes, Ananas.	*Champagne.* Heidsieck Monopol, Jules Mumm, carte rose, Rœderer, carte blanche, Giesler Goldlack.

Mocha Coffee.

◁BANQUET▷

TENDERED TO

BISHOP LOUGHLIN ᴮʸ ᴛʜᴇ PRIESTS OF HIS DIOCESE,

OCTOBER 18, 1890.

Huîtres en Coquilles.

Sauterne.

SOUPES.

Consommé aux Quenelles,   Tortue Verte à l'Anglaise.

Amontillado.

HORS D'ŒUVRES.

Coquilles St. Jacques,   Saucisson de Lyon,
Sardines,   Céleri,   Radis,   Olives.

POISSONS.

Saumon,   Sauce Hollandaise,   Concombres,
Pommes Quélins.

Médoc.

RELEVÉS.

Dinde Braisée à la Régence,   Haricots Verts Français.

ENTRÉES.

Filet de Bœuf à la Richelieu,   Petits Pois Nature,
Riz de Veau en Caisses Béarnaises,   Asperges en Branches.

St. Julien.

SORBET.

Punch Romain.

RÔTI.

Squabs de Philadelphie,   Chicorie et Laitue.

Pomard.

ENTREMETS SUCRÉS.

Pudding de Cabinet,   Gateaux Assortis Mendiants,
Glaces de Fantaisie.

Heidsieck Sec.,
G. H. Mumm's E. D.

DESSERT.

Fruits de Saison,   Fromages,   Café Noir,   Cigares.

◁BANQUET▷

TENDERED TO

Rt. Rev. JOHN LOUGHLIN, D.D., Bishop of Brooklyn,

BY THE LAITY ON THE OCCASION OF HIS

GOLDEN JUBILEE,

OCTOBER 20, 1890.

Huîtres en Coquilles. *Haut Sauternes.*
SOUPES. *Impérial.*
Consommé aux Quenelles, Tortue Verte.
HORS D'ŒUVRES.
Variés, Bouchées Duchesses.
POISSONS. *Rudesheimer.*
Filet de Sole Farci au Vin Blanc, Saumon, Sauce Genevoise,
Salade de Concombres.
RELEVÉS. *Château Laroze.*
Selle de Venaison, Gelée de Groseille,
Filet de Bœuf, aux Champignons Nouveaux,
Pommes Duchesses, Petits Pois à la Française.
ENTRÉES. *Moet et Chandon,*
Terrapène à la Maryland, *Brut Impérial.*
Timbales Mathilde. *Perrier Jouët E. D.,*
Special.
LÉGUMES.
Asperges, Sauce Hollandaise.
PUNCH. *Cigarettes.*
Loughlin.
RÔTIS. *Chambertin.*
Perdreaux sur Canapé, Bécassines au Cresson,
Salade de Chicorée.
ENTREMETS SUCRÉS. *Pommery Dry.*
Savarins à l'Impératrice. *G. H. Mumm E. D.*
DESSERT.
Glaces en Surprises,
Fruits Glacés, Gâteaux, Petits Fours, Cosaques, Bonbons,
Fruits de Saison.
FROMAGES.
Café Noir,
Apollinaris, Cigars,
Lemon Soda, Ginger Ale, Liqueurs.

HAIL AND FAREWELL BANQUET

TENDERED TO THE

INCOMING AND OUTGOING JUSTICES

OF THE

CITY COURT OF NEW YORK.

The Hon. FITZSIMMONS,   The Hon. NEWBERGER,
The Hon. McADAM,   The Hon. GIEGERICH,

By their Associates.

HUÎTRES.   *Chablis.*

POTAGES.   *Amontillado.*

Consommé Adelina,   Tortue Verte Claire.

HORS D'ŒUVRE.   *Pontet Canet.*

Timbales à la Talleyrand.

POISSON.   *Liebfraumilch.*

Aiguillettes de Bass,   Dieppoise,
Pommes de terre Anglaises,   Concombres.

RELEVÉS.   *G. H. Mumm's.*

Selle d'Antilope à la Grainville,   Asperges.

ENTRÉES.   *G. H. Mumm's.*

Filet de Poulet à la Lucullus,   Petits Pois Parisiennes,
Terrapène à la Maryland,   Sorbet Tosca.   *Cigarettes.*

RÔTIS.   *Chambertin.*

Canvasback Duck,   Salade de Laitue.

ENTREMETS SUCRÉS.   *Pommery Dry.*

Poires à la Richelieu.

FROMAGES.   *G. H. Mumm's.*

Glaces Fantaisie,   Fruits,   Petits Fours,
Café,   Liqueurs.

LUNDI, LE 22 DÉCEMBRE, 1890.
DELMONICO'S.

ANNUAL BANQUET,

New York Board of Trade and Transportation,

DELMONICO'S, THURSDAY, JAN. 29, 1891.

HUÎTRES. *Haut Sauternes.*

POTAGES. *Amontillado.*
Consommé Dubelloy, Bisque de Crevettes.

HORS D'ŒUVRE. *Batailley.*
Timbales Ecarlatte.

POISSON. *Marcobrunner.*
Saumon de l'Orégon, Hollandaise Vert Pie,
Pommes de Terre Duchesses.

RELEVÉ. *Vve. Clicquot.*
Filet de Bœuf aux Olives Farcies, Choux Fleurs au Gratin.

ENTRÉES. *G. H. Mumm's.*
Poularde à la Chevreuse, Petits Pois à l'Anglaise,
Caisses de Ris de Veau Grammont,
Haricots Panachés.

SORBET IMPÉRIAL.

RÔTI. *Chambertin.*
Canards à Tête Rouge (Froid),
Terrine de Foies Gras à la Gelée, Salade de Laitue.

ENTREMET DE DOUCEUR. *Perrier Jouët.*
Pouding Favorite, Pièces Montées,
Glaces Fantaisie,
Fruits, Petits Fours, Café.

At this banquet the Hon. WILLIAM WINDOM, Secretary of the Treasury, died.

Introduction to Mixed Drinks:

Containing Hints to the Professional Barkeeper and General Remarks to the Public.

Introduction to Mixed Drinks.

To those who do not find the following useful in its details for their own use, I express my congratulations and esteem as a business associate. To those who do find it a guide I wish to express my assurance that they will find this work an absolutely and indispensably correct one to work by, provided they understand and practice it.

You may travel all over the country, and you will find my practice a good one. In discharging your duties you will find many little hints you will not be able to practice for not having the facilities to do so, but I may say I have at least shown you how it ought to be made and executed. It must be left to your own judgment to follow the directions given herein the best way you know of, and leave out what ought to be left out, because your position does not offer you the opportunity. I have mentioned in this work everything that is necessary for a theoretical experience. It should be borne in mind: Not everybody can advance so as to become an artist in tending bar, but we all should learn, and try to improve by all means that are offered. I am far from believing it possible to become a practical man by simply studying this book, but while doing so, you will get an essential and true idea of how to become a valuable man in this line of business. Every man can educate himself and acquire all the knowledge necessary for tending bar, provided he takes enough interest and wants to make it a business. Practical knowledge cannot be acquired except by actual work and experience.

An inexpert cook never will become an artist nor a *chef de cuisine* by simply reading a book on cookery, no matter by whom or how intelligently written, and no man can ever become an artist behind the bar by simply looking into this book or possessing it. A great deal of ingenuity and taste is required on the part of a *chef* in an important position, and the same is required on the part of a man in the capacity of a bartender. He, having a position of responsibility, must be a man of original ideas, a man who is proud of his work and who tries to discharge his duties with credit to himself, his employer, and the guest he waits on. Originality is the key to success. Therefore, always try to work accordingly; make a change in the old system, if you see it needs improvement; introduce it to your guests instead of being taught by them what to do. A bartender ought to be leading and not to be led. An actor must understand for himself how to amuse his audience and how to gain a reputation: he never would succeed by simply following another man's guidance.

The situation of a barkeeper gives the holder the chance of studying human nature. A man fit for the position, and consequently a keen observer—for one thing cannot be separated from the other—will be able to tell a man's character very soon, as far as conduct, education, language, and general *savoir-vivre* are concerned.

Such a situation is a better teacher of human nature than any book howsoever, and by whomsoever it may be written. "Tell me what you drink and I will tell you who you are." The tastes and habits of your different customers appear to you so plain, that you have to take an interest in this study of human nature.

As a general rule you will find that only a little part of drinking is done by one individual. A gentleman either brings his company with him or he expects to find it in the barroom. It is in drinking as it is in eating: very few want to enjoy their drinks by themselves.

As to my individual belief, all men are born equal, with a heart full of honesty; I cannot believe any one might think otherwise. If any one grows up to become different, it is the fault of his surroundings or his own carelessness. How any one can lie without knowing what he does it for, I cannot comprehend. Thus with me! Many a time I have been asked concerning mixed drinks: What do you think of them in regard to their effect and result to the stomach? Many a time I have heard the complaint, mixed drinks make a person sick; consequently we do not believe in them; we think them to be bad and a failure. Patience, my dear patrons! Most cheerfully I give the following answer: Drinking is a luxury, water and milk excepted, and any man will admit this fact who is not a slave to drinking. First of all, if you make a mixed drink, your honesty must force you to use pure articles only. Suppose you need for your drink three or four ingredients; take every article genuine but one, and you will spoil the entire drink by the one that is not genuine. Therefore, order mixed drinks only in reliable places.

Secondly: Never order a mixed drink when you are in a hurry; you can get a well-mixed drink only when you devote the time absolutely necessary to prepare it.

Thirdly: The mixer ought to be careful not to use too much of one ingredient and too little of another. Do not get too much water in your drink when you prepare drinks with ice; find the suitable temperature, not too warm nor too cold; chiefly, however, be careful in your measurements, and compare a plain drink in its size with your mixed one.

Mixing drinks might be compared to music; an orchestra will produce good music, provided all players are artists; but have only one or two inferior musicians in your band, and you may be convinced they will spoil the entire harmony.

A man who is a slave to drinking will always prefer something strong, even if less palatable, and the effect is generally harmful to his brain; whereas the man who believes in mixed drinks may hurt his stomach, in case he drinks too much; but even this too much will never reach the quantity of the former.

It must be borne in mind: Drinking is an art, and it requires practice to know how to drink, what to drink, and when to drink. Drinking is like eating. Who but a cannibal would not prefer his viands prepared in a palatable form? That fancy cooking is not injurious, we have full proof of; we know of aged people of the past and of the present who spent a little fortune in having their dishes made to suit their taste. As good eating depends on the cook, so good drinking on the expert barkeeper.

A distinguished Englishman, Mr. T., one day told me: "We do not have much mixed drinks in our country." Whereupon I asked him: "Why do your countrymen mix ale with porter, or Bass ale with ginger ale?" "Well, it makes the drink more pleasant to the taste." I needed no more answer.

A man gets tired of good company, of good friends, or even of his best girl—why should we wonder at seeing him getting tired of mixed drinks? I cannot help stating the fact that our drinking capacity is increasing, compared with former times. Not everybody is capable of criticising and appreciating a good drink, more so a mixed one. Never smoke when you want to enjoy a fine drink, nor chew; never drink anything mixed when you do not feel well. For medical purposes, plain drinks are preferable.

When I began my business as bartender, I was only a boy and hardly able to keep up with the demands of my employer; I remembered this often enough afterwards; yet the imagination on my part was at that time like that of the rest of boys of the same age. But with the advance in age, this imagination faded, for it had to; and now I began to learn. A period of a few years passed and I began to believe I knew something; undoubtedly I did, but how little! and every day convinces me more and more how much there is to be learned, although I have given particular care to this business close on to thirty years.

How often a man will overestimate himself, because he happens to be successful, as well as another one will undervalue his dexterity because good luck did not favor him. Perhaps you think I was born with a fortune waiting for me; I was, but I was not to keep it, and only my misfortune in younger years is the cause, and has ever since been, that made me work hard and seek new ideas. There is no more reason for a well-off man to give up his ambition than there is for another, who did not meet with success, to despair. Surely it is a nice, pleasant feeling for any one to be born rich; but to be born with a silver spoon in the mouth and to die with a fortune behind you, without having shown that you accomplished something of value through your daily toils and labors—no! I would rather be a dog than a man without ambition and a record of toil.

My dear readers! Never was I guilty of not enjoying myself at every opportunity after business hours, and I never will let the time pass by without doing so hereafter. It is a pleasure to me to enjoy the labor, the skill and the talent of others, and I know how to value and appreciate it, but still my greatest pleasure is to amuse others; and you will find, "True happiness is gained by making others happy." Often have I done extra work to amuse my friends, for the pleasure I felt was ample reward.

I would mention right here some of my little extra doings, different from the usual way. When you are not pushed for time, while you are making mixed drinks, cool your glasses with ice before you serve your drink; in serving a strained drink, you begin with serving a glass of ice-water; then fill your glass, into which you are to strain your drink, with ice. You may place your glasses together in the form of a pyramid and ornament your structure with fruits and flowers. Now begin to prepare your drink. By following these hints you will accomplish several purposes: Firstly, you will please the eye of your customer; secondly, you will have thoroughly cooled glasses; thirdly, you will not need to wipe your glasses dry, etc.

On a hot summer day you will find such little extras to a great advantage to the business practically, *i. e.*, financially. A drink well served is worth two that lack in presentation.

When a drink is made with ice and then strained, there should be nothing left in the glass but the liquid; the fruit would hinder you in drinking, it would touch the mustache; if you want to eat it you cannot get it out, and the fruit has lost its natural aroma; fruit ought, consequently, to be presented separately, if it is desired on your guest's part.

Very different it is when you have a drink in which the ice is to remain; in this case use plenty of fruits, as it is pleasing to the eye and allows your guest to eat it if he likes.

Reasons Why Men Drink.

MEN drink to quench thirst, on account of a drink's effect, to get an appetite, to promote digestion, to enjoy its taste, for curiosity, from habit, because of discouragement, on account of ambition, to forget poverty, to show their riches, because of sickness, because they do not feel well, for the purpose of learning, to dispel sorrow. This one wants to warm himself; that one is overheated and wants to get cool; one has lost in Wall Street; another's shares have gone up; one man's best girl went back on him; another is going to marry the best girl in town; one drinks behind the door, another in a public place. Some men will drink out of pure style; they want to show their diamonds and jewelry, their costly clothes, and mainly their money. But most men will drink because it is " business." I remember a circumstance that occurred between a diamond broker of Maiden Lane and myself. One fine morning a customer entered his store to buy goods, but the broker did not succeed in selling, when all at once the idea struck him, "A nice drink might bring him to terms." He invited his customer and up they came to the bar. With a twinkle in his eye he ordered "Two of those famous Sans Soucis." I went to work and built up the glasses, à l'Eiffel tower, with all the necessary fruits and flowers, and after having received a pleasant compliment from my guest, I saw them going down to the store once more. As I was afterwards informed, the broker sold his customer $10,000 worth of goods with ease.

How to Start.

CLEAN the top of your counter first, remove all utensils from under the counter and place them on the top; clean your bench. Before beginning with your glassware, add a little salt to the water as it will help in polishing your glasses. Fill all your liquor bottles, pack your working boxes with fine ice, cut up the fruit for immediate use, clean your silverware. Fill your ice-boxes with ice. Afterward clean your back bar.

As an appropriate suit behind the bar I would mention the following: a pair of black trousers, a long, white apron, a white shirt, a white collar, a black tie, a white vest, and a white coat; care should be taken to have the suit fit well; have the sleeves of your coat cut, that you may button it tight; this will prevent its getting soiled and worn out; never have your suit starched.

Glassware.

IN selecting your glassware, choose perfectly white color, also for your bottles, as they look much more inviting. To keep them clean, use egg-shells, salt, paper, or chopped ice. It should be remembered that shot is very poisonous and scratches the glass. Soda ought also to be avoided. Use only plain but good glassware, it being the best.

Fruits.

Lemons.—Lemons intended for squeezing should be peeled before using. The juice ought not to be older than a day. It must be strained thoroughly. Lime-juice may be mixed with lemon-juice; the mixture is cheaper and better. The fresh lemon-peel is very useful for flavoring and decorating the drinks.

Oranges.—A medium size of dark-colored ones is the best for squeezing, as well as cutting up. Use from six to twelve oranges, according to the demand of the business; peel them and take them apart carefully; place them in a punch-bowl, add some fine sugar, pour either Rhine wine, sherry wine or brandy over it; let it stand in a cold place from three to six hours, and serve a piece to your customer after the drink, and you will find it will be appreciated.

The Delicious Pineapple.—Pineapple may be used in the same way as oranges, the juice or syrup being almost indispensable.

Choice Grapes.—To make a drink of inviting appearance choice grapes are necessary, for decorating as well as simply presenting.

In addition to these fruits, a few others ought to be

kept on hand: Strawberries, raspberries, blackberries and cherries. They may be prepared the same way as the other fruits.

Never handle fruits with your fingers, but use a fancy fruit-fork.

Canned Fruits.

AT a time when there are no fresh fruits to be had, canned goods may be taken instead of them. The juice or the syrup of them lends a very aromatic flavor to drinks—such as cobblers, punches, sours, fizzes and lemonades. You also may present a little of these fruits to your customers.

To persons who drink strong liquors, the use of fruits is of a much greater advantage than lunch. The proper way of serving such little relishes is to put them in a separate little glass, or present on a fork or a toothpick.

Further Instructions.

NEVER allow yourself to be idle behind the bar; be ready to serve at once when a customer enters. When a drink is ordered that requires water, fill your glass with fine ice, and pour over it water out of a pitcher in full view of your guest. This rule must necessarily be carried out in performing every one of your duties. A bottle never must be more than half empty. For strong drinks, always serve two glasses—one for the drink, the other for the water. Serve sherry and port wine in their respective glasses only; never do it in whiskey tumblers.

For shaking drinks with the shaker, use only a mixing-tumbler; by using goblets you will soil your clothes, and the goblets might break. Shake your drink well; without that you never will get a first-class drink. This has special reference to such drinks as fizzes, milk punches, egg-noggs, frappés, and similar drinks, containing sugar. Good mixing is a hard work; but without good mixing you spoil the best liquor.

In serving your guest, be pleasant, but quiet. Never commence to converse, only answer questions. Never listen to conversation held between your guests, nor hold any conversation behind the bar with your co-workers. In receiving money, avoid mistakes; in returning change, be careful. Observe who orders drinks, and, if you give a check, hand it to the right person; mistakes in this respect will often lead to disputes. Treat every one respectfully, but do not lose your dignity in the proper place. You can do this only by using good and selected language, and be conservative in your actions.

As we mention syrup or gum so often, we think it a necessity to call your attention to the way of making and using it.

Take an enameled pot, of about half a gallon; put in this one and a half quarts of water and two pounds of loaf-sugar; let this boil over a slow fire; stir now and then, and skim well; if too thick, add a little boiling water, and strain into a bottle. It ought to be kept in a cold place. Do not prepare too large quantities, as it is best to have it fresh.

Rock-candy gum is prepared in the same way. Cocktail gum should be absolutely white.

Mixed Drinks:

Containing

Sours,	Temperance Drinks,
Cocktails,	Cobblers,
Punches (for the bar use),	Fizzes,
Lemonades,	Diverse.

NOTE.—Whenever in any recipe you find ½, or ⅔, or ⅙, etc., it means ⅓, etc., of the final drink. A dash being no definite measure, I must leave it to the mixer's good judgment to suit his customers' taste.

Mixed Drinks.

1. Jack Frost Whiskey Sour.

Into a mixing-glass squeeze the juice of half a lemon,
> 1 barspoonful of sugar,
> 1 fresh egg,
> 1 pony of fresh cream,
> 1 drink of apple whiskey.

Fill your glass with cracked ice and shake thoroughly; strain into a high, thin glass, and fill the balance with imported seltzer.

2. Sour à la Créole.

The juice of a large lime in a large glass,
> a barspoonful of fine sugar,
> a dash of seltzer; mix this well;
> ½ drink of Santa Cruz rum,
> ½ drink of Jamaica rum.

Mix this well, fill your glass with fine ice, ornament with fruits in season, put a little ice-cream on top, and serve.

3. Whiskey Sour à la Guillaume.

A large glass with fine ice,
> the juice of half a lemon,
> 3 dashes of gum,
> a drink of whiskey,
> 2 spoonfuls of cream.

Shake this, strain, and serve.

4. The Delicious Sour.

A goblet with the juice of a lime,
        a squirt of seltzer,
        a spoonful of sugar,
        ½ of apple-jack,
        ½ of peach brandy,
        the white of an egg.
Fill your glass with ice, shake well, strain, and serve.

5. Oriental Brandy Sour.

Into a mixing-glass squeeze the juice of half a lemon,
        a barspoonful of sugar,
        the juice of half an orange,
        the white of an egg,
        a drink of peach brandy.
Fill the glass with cracked ice, shake to the freezing-point, strain into a fancy glass, and serve.

6. Whiskey Sour.

A goblet with the juice of half a lemon or lime in the bottom,
        a squirt of seltzer,
        a little sugar; mix this;
        ⅔ full of ice,
        a drink of whiskey; mix this well.
Strain, and serve.

7. Whiskey Daisy.

It is made as a whiskey sour; only put a dash of some cordial on top, such as chartreuse or curaçao.

8. Absinthe Cocktail.

A goblet of shaved ice,
   2 dashes of maraschino,
   1 dash of bitters (orange),
   1 dash of anisette,
   1 pony of absinthe.
Stir very well, strain into a cocktail glass, and serve.

9. The Angelus.

Fill a large glass two-thirds full of fine ice,
   1 dash of gum,
   1 dash of absinthe,
   a little vino vermouth,
   1 pony of Old Tom gin,
   2 dashes of orange bitters,
   2 dashes of curaçao.
Stir well, and strain into a fancy glass.

10. The Anticipation.

A glass with fine ice,
   1 dash of absinthe,
   2 dashes of gum,
   ½ of sherry wine,
   ½ of vino vermouth.
Freeze this well; strain and serve.

11. The Bitter-Sweet Cocktail.

A glass with ice,
   ⅓ drink of kümmel,
   ⅓ drink of vino vermouth,
   4 dashes of absinthe,
   1 dash of bitters (orange),
   3 dashes of gum,
   1 dash of anisette.
Stir, strain, and serve.

12. The Great Appetizer.

Fill a glass with ice,
> 3 dashes of gum,
> ½ pony of absinthe,
> 2 dashes of bitters (calisaya),
> 1 dash of orange bitters,
> 1 dash of vino vermouth.

Stir this well, strain, and serve.

13. Bon-Appetit.

A goblet two-thirds full of fine ice,
> 2 dashes of gum,
> 1 dash of bitters,
> 1 dash of absinthe,
> ⅔ of vino vermouth,
> ⅓ of sherry wine.

Stir well, strain, and serve.

14. Appetizer à l'Italienne.

> ⅔ of vino vermouth,
> ⅓ of Fernet branca,
> 1 dash of absinthe,
> 2 dashes of gum.

A little ice in the glass, stir well, strain, and serve.

15. L'Aurore.

A goblet filled with fine ice,
> 1 dash of gum,
> 2 dashes of orange bitters,
> ⅓ of vino vermouth,
> ⅔ of Old Tom gin,
> 1 dash of absinthe,
> 1 dash of maraschino.

Stir, strain, and serve with a little fruit.

16. The Beginner.

A goblet with fine ice,
        2 dashes of gum,
        2 dashes of orange bitters,
        1 dash of absinthe,
        ½ of French vermouth,
        ½ of Russian kümmel.
Stir this well, strain, and serve.

17. The Brain-Duster.

Into a mixing-tumbler squeeze the juice of a lime,
        2 dashes of gum,
        1 pony of absinthe,
        2 dashes of vino vermouth,
        2 dashes of sherry wine.
Fill your glass with ice, stir, strain, and serve.

18. Exquisite.

A goblet with 2 dashes of gum,
        1 dash of bitters,
        1 dash of absinthe,
        ⅔ of vino vermouth,
        ⅓ of Russian kümmel,
        1 dash of crême de roses.
Fill your glass with ice, stir, strain, and serve.

19. The First One.

A goblet with fine ice,
        2 dashes of gum,
        ½ pony of crême de menthe,
        1 pony of Old Tom gin,
        1 dash of orange bitters.
Squeeze the juice of a lemon-peel to it; stir well, strain, and serve.

20. The Gladstone.

Fill a tumbler half-full with fine ice,
    2 dashes of gum,
    a little maraschino,
    2 dashes of bitters,
    1 dash of absinthe,
    1 drink of whiskey,
    1 dash of Jamaica rum,
    1 dash of Russian kümmel.
Stir well and strain into a cocktail glass.

21. Holland Gin Cocktail.

A goblet filled with fine ice,
    2 dashes of gum,
    1 dash of absinthe,
    1 drink of Holland gin,
    2 dashes of orange bitters.
(1 dash of green chartreuse may be added.)
Stir this well, strain, and serve.

22. Holland's Pride.

A mixing glass ⅔ full of ice,
    3 dashes of gum.
    2 dashes of bitters,
    1 dash of absinthe,
    ⅔ of Holland gin,
    ⅓ of vino vermouth.
Stir well, strain, and serve.

23. Manhattan Cocktail.

Half a tumblerful of cracked ice,
    2 dashes of gum,
    2 dashes of bitters,
    1 dash of absinthe,
    ⅔ drink of whiskey,
    ⅓ drink of vino vermouth.
(A little maraschino may be added.)
Stir this well, strain, and serve.

24. Imperial Opal.

A mixing-glass ⅔ filled with fine ice,
> 1 pony of absinthe,
> 1 dash of anisette,
> 1 dash of chartreuse (yellow).

Shake this to the freezing-point; strain into a cocktail glass; drop a little crême de roses in the centre, and serve

25. The Opal.

A goblet with ice,
> 2 dashes of gum,
> 1 pony of absinthe,
> 1 dash of maraschino.

Stir well, strain into a cocktail glass; pour a little crême de menthe in the centre, which will go to the bottom, and serve.

26. The Preserver.

A large glass ⅔ full of fine ice,
> 1 dash of bitters,
> 1 dash of absinthe,
> ⅔ of vino vermouth,
> ⅙ of anisette,
> ⅙ of curaçao.

Mix well, strain into a fancy glass, and present.

27. Soda Cocktail.

A large glass with a spoonful of sugar,
> squeeze a little oil of the peel of a lemon on it,
> a little fine ice,
> 2 dashes of bitters.

Pour in a bottle of plain soda slowly with your left hand, while you stir it with your right hand, and present; strain if desired.

28. Tom Gin Cocktail.

A goblet filled with ice,
    2 small dashes of gum,
    1 dash of absinthe,
    1 drink of Old Tom gin,
    2 dashes of orange bitters.
(A dash of green chartreuse may be added.)
Stir well, strain, and serve.

29. Club Cocktail.

Half a glassful of ice,
    2 dashes of gum,
    ⅔ of Old Tom gin,
    ⅓ of vino vermouth,
    2 dashes of orange bitters,
    1 dash of green chartreuse.
Stir well, strain, and serve.

30. Vermouth Cocktail.

A glass with some fine ice,
    1 dash of bitters,
    2 dashes of maraschino,
    1 dash of absinthe,
    1 drink of vino vermouth.
Stir to the freezing-point, and strain into a cocktail glass.

31. The Weeper's Joy.

A goblet ⅔ full of fine ice,
    3 dashes of gum,
    ½ pony of absinthe,
    ½ pony of vino vermouth,
    ½ pony of kümmel,
    1 dash of curaçao.
Stir very well, and strain into a cocktail glass.

32. Whiskey Cocktail.

Half a glassful of fine ice,
>   squeeze a little lemon-peel over it,
>   3 dashes of gum,
>   2 dashes of bitters,
>   1 dash of absinthe,
>   1 drink of whiskey.

Stir this well, strain and serve.

33. Hot Apple Toddy.

A lump of sugar dissolved in half a glass of boiling water,
>   a drink of apple whiskey.

Add a piece of a roasted apple, if you wish, and serve with a little nutmeg.

34. Hot Beef-Tea.

Break an egg in the bottom of a cup; beat it well;
>   a drink of sherry,
>   a spoonful of beef-tea.

Fill the balance with boiling water; stir well, season to taste, and serve.

35. Hot Benefactor.

A hot punch-glass with 2 or 3 lumps of sugar,
>   ½ glass of boiling water to dissolve,
>   ⅔ of Chianti,
>   ⅓ of Jamaica rum,
>   1 slice of lemon.

Grate a little nutmeg on top, and serve.

36. The Old Style of Blue Blazer.

The same as a hot Scotch, only take a hot silver mug, pour in your hot Scotch and light it; leave it burning for about 2 minutes, while you pour it into another hot mug, and *vice versa;* then serve.

37. Hot Brandy.

A hot glass with 2 lumps of sugar, well dissolved in ½ glass of boiling water,
> ⅔ of brandy,
> ⅓ of Burgundy.

Mix this well, and add a slice of orange.

38. Hong Kong Punch.

The juice of a lime, and 3 dashes of pineapple-juice in the bottom of a hot, thin glass,
> a spoonful of sugar,
> a cup of strong boiling tea,
> a drink of Jamaica rum,
> 2 dashes of brandy,
> a piece of sliced lemon.

If not hot enough add a little hot water. (You may add a dash of maraschino.)

39. Lait de Poule.

(FOR THE SICK.)

Break the yolks of 2 fresh eggs in the bottom of a glass, beat this up well with a spoonful of sugar, and 3 spoonfuls of orange-flower extract, until the eggs begin to look white; while you stir with one hand, add a glass of hot water, a pony of brandy, and stir well before serving.

40. Hot Italian Lemonade.

The juice of half a lemon and of half an orange,
> a large spoonful of sugar.

Fill your glass nearly up with boiling water; add a little Chianti; stir, and serve with a little nutmeg on top.

41. Ladies' Hot Punch.

A hot glass half full of boiling water, with 2 lumps of sugar well dissolved,
>½ drink of sherry wine,
>½ drink of port wine; mix this well;
>1 slice of orange, and a little nutmeg on the top.

42. Hot Orange Lemonade, with Brandy.

In a large wineglass squeeze the juice of a lime, and the juice of an orange,
>a large spoonful of sugar; dissolve this well;
>1 pony of brandy; mix well.

While you stir with one hand, fill your glass with boiling milk slowly.

43. Hot Red Wine Punch.

A large, hot glass with the juice of half a lemon in the bottom,
>3 lumps of sugar,
>½ glass of boiling water; dissolve this well;
>a glass of claret,
>a dash of Jamaica rum.

Mix this thoroughly; add a slice of an orange, and a little cinnamon.

44. Hot Scotch.

A hot glass half full of boiling water,
>a lump or two of sugar; dissolve well;
>a drink of Scotch whiskey; mix this.

If desired, a little lemon-peel, and a little nutmeg.

45. A Sure Relief.

A punch-glass half full of boiling water,
  2 lumps of sugar; dissolve well;
  1 pony of peppermint,
  1 dash of Jamaica ginger,
  1 pony of brandy,
  1 dash of raspberry syrup,
  the peel of a little lemon, and serve.

46. Black Rose.

A hot glass with 2 lumps of sugar,
  3 or 4 cloves,
  a piece of cinnamon,
  ½ glass of boiling water; mix well.
Fill your glass with Assmannshäuser, and add a piece of orange.

47. Scotch Delight.

A hot glass with 2 lumps of sugar,
  ½ glass of boiling water; dissolve well;
  ½ of Scotch whiskey,
  ½ of Irish whiskey,
  1 dash of claret.
Mix well, and add a little lemon-peel.

48. Fancy Hot Sherry.

A hot glass half full of boiling water,
  2 small lumps of sugar; dissolve well;
  a drink of sherry,
  a dash of port wine,
  ½ slice of lemon,
  a little cinnamon on the top.

49. Swedish Punch.

A hot glass half filled with boiling water; add to this enough Swedish punch essence to make it palatable; add a little nutmeg if desired.

50. Hot Spiced Rum.

A hot, thin glass half filled with boiling water,
    1 or 2 lumps of sugar; dissolve this well;
    a drink of Jamaica rum,
    a dash of claret,
    a small piece of butter,
    a roasted cracker,
    2 or 3 cloves, and serve.

51. Base-Ball Lemonade.

A fresh egg in the bottom of a glass,
    the juice of a lemon,
    a spoonful of sugar,
    a little fine ice,
    $\frac{1}{3}$ of water,
    $\frac{2}{3}$ of milk.
Shake this very well, and serve.

52. Bavaroise à l'Eau.

A large bar-glass,
    $\frac{1}{3}$ full of capillaire syrup,
    1 barspoonful of orange-flower water.
Fill the glass with boiling water or tea, squeeze the oil of a little lemon-peel on the top.

53. Bavaroise Mexicaine.

Put 1 barspoonful of pulverized sugar and the yolk of an egg in a large glass; stir it well with a spoon,
    1 pony of old Jamaica rum.
Fill the balance with boiling milk while stirring.

54. Italian Lemonade.

The juice of half a peeled lemon and orange,
a large spoonful of fine sugar,
the glass full of ice.
Fill your glass with water, shake this well, add a little dash of Chianti; ornament with fruits and ice-cream.

55. Raspberry Lemonade, with Wine.

The juice of a lime or a lemon,
a spoonful of sugar,
the juice of 1 dozen raspberries.
Fill your glass with ice, add a glass of sherry or port wine, fill your glass up with water, shake well, ornament with fruits and ice-cream, and serve with a straw.

56. Soda Lemonade.

The juice of ½ lemon,
1 spoonful of sugar,
dissolve well in a large glass,
2 or 3 lumps of ice.
Pour in your plain soda with the left hand while you stir with the right, and serve.

57. Seltzer Lemonade.

It is made the same way, only use Seltzer instead of soda.

58. Strawberry Lemonade.

The juice of a lemon,
1 spoonful of sugar in a large glass.
the juice of 1 dozen strawberries.
Fill your glass one-third full of ice and the balance with milk; shake this very well and strain into a long, thin glass.

59. Violet Lemonade.

Mix a tablespoonful of violet syrup and a spoonful of sugar with the juice of ½ lemon in a glass of water (cold); this is a very pleasant drink, especially adapted against headache and nervous diseases.

60. Another.

In a large glass the juice of half a lemon,
        a spoonful of pineapple syrup,
        a spoonful of sugar,
        3 dashes of crême de violet.

Fill your glass with ice, shake well, ornament with ice-cream and berries, and serve with a straw.

61. Lemonade Parfait.

Put the rind of twelve peeled lemons in three quarts of boiling water; press their juice, after cooling, into the fluid; add one and a half pounds of pulverized sugar, three-fourths of a quart of Rhine wine and 1 pint of boiled milk; stir well and strain through canton flannel.

62. Apricot Sherbet.

From three pounds of ripe apricots select the largest ones, put the smaller ones with three gills of water in a stone pot, let boil until the pits fall out, strain the juice through canton flannel and squeeze the fruits well; boil the juice with one pound of sugar to a thick syrup; boil the larger ones soft in one and a half quarts of water until they burst. Take them out and remove the pits. Strain the water, in which they were boiled, into a bowl, add the syrup, put the fruit in, cut in two, with some lumps of ice, and season with almond essence.

63. Bavaroise au Chocolat.

Put in a vessel partly filled with boiling water a pot with one quart of milk: break five ounces of vanilla chocolate and drop it into the milk; stir continually, but never let the milk boil; hand out the glasses, put in every one a tablespoonful of sugar syrup and fill in the chocolate concoction; serve it hot

64. Bavaroise à l'Italienne.

Put two teaspoonfuls of pulverized sugar and a bit of powdered cinnamon in a glass; add one-half of coffee and the other half of chocolate dissolved in boiling water; serve it hot.

65. Bavaroise au Lait.

Take a large glass, fill it to one-third with capillaire syrup, add a teaspoonful of orange-flower water and fill it up with boiling milk.

66. Bilberry Lemonade.

One pint of bilberry-juice is mixed with two quarts of cold water; add one and a half pounds of powdered sugar, in case the juice should not have been sweetened before; mix well and serve cold.

67. Cherry Lemonade.

Put two pounds of sour cherries in a tureen, mash them with a wooden spoon and pour two and a half or three quarts of boiling water over it. A small portion of the pits is cracked, put them in the tureen, cover well and let soak about three hours; filter; mix with a quart of sugar refined and cleared to syrup and let it get cold. A spoonful of St. Croix rum or arrack increases the fine taste of this lemonade exceedingly.

68. Cherry Lemonade.

(FOR THE SICK.)

Mash one pound of dried sour cherries, pits and all, and boil it in one quart of water with the rind of half a lemon and a small stick of cinnamon slowly half an hour; strain through flannel, sweeten with sugar to taste and keep it in a bottle for use.

69. Cherry Sherbet.

From three pounds of sour cherries a number of the largest and finest are selected; the juice of the rest is pressed through a cloth into a pot and heated to boiling with one pound of sugar; the selected large cherries are boiled soft in one to one and a half quarts of water; take them from the fire, lift them out carefully, put them in a bowl with one quart of the water in which they were boiled and with their juice, add a few drops of rose or orange-flower essence and a few lumps of ice, and serve.

70. Citronelle.

Use a large glass with some fine ice,
⅓ glass of green tea,
⅓ glass of black tea,
⅓ glass of lemon syrup.
Shake well, and serve.

71. Currant Lemonade.

Half a quart of fresh currant-juice is mixed with one quart of cold water and one pound of sugar and strained through a flannel; or you take currant syrup; mix one pound of it with the juice of a lemon and one and one-fourth quarts of cold water.

72. English Milk Lemonade.

Peel the rind of two fine lemons very thinly, squeeze the juice of the lemons, cut the rind into small pieces, and let it soak for about twelve hours; filter; mix with two pounds of sugar refined to syrup, a bottle of sherry, and two and a half quarts of fresh, boiling milk. Clear the lemonade by filtering often enough through a flannel bag, and a very cooling summer-drink will crown your efforts.

73. Fig Sherbet.

Cut off the stems of two pounds of large dried figs; pierce each with a wooden pick several times; infuse with one and a half quarts of boiling water over night, strain, add a few drops of orange-flower water, some lumps of ice, and the figs, and serve.

74. Gooseberry Lemonade.

To one quart of water add one pint of gooseberry-juice, and one pound of pulverized sugar.

75. Ice Lemonade.

Well-prepared orange or raspberry lemonade is filled into a bottle; dig this into cracked ice, and serve after three-quarters of an hour, when little lumps of ice are forming in the lemonade.

76. Imperial.

Place in a large, well-warmed pot, one ounce of cremor tartari, the rind of three very thinly peeled lemons, one and a half pounds of sugar; pour over it two and a half quarts of boiling water, cover the pot well, and let it stand an hour in a temperate place; stir now and then; put it on ice, and decant it very carefully.

77. Boiled Lemonade.

Put the rind of two thinly peeled lemons in a tea-pot; then remove the white skin of the fruit, cut them into very thin slices, remove the seeds; put the slices likewise in the pot, and add one pint of boiling water; cover the pot well and let it soak for about ten minutes; drink it hot after sweetening with sugar to taste.

(This lemonade can be very warmly recommended in cases of cold, before going to bed.)

78. Lemonade Gazeuse.

Half an ounce of carbonate of magnesia is ground in one pint of water; fill the milky fluid into a glass bottle, add half an ounce of crystallized citric acid, and close the bottle air-tight. After twelve hours filter the fluid into another bottle, in which you first place one-fourth ounce of citric acid and two ounces of sugar syrup; fill the bottle up with fresh water; cork well; fasten the cork with twine, and shake in order to mix the syrup with the water, and to dissolve the citric acid, which then sets free the carbonic acid in the carbonate of magnesia; which acid makes the lemonade sparkle.

79. Orange Lemonade.

Take one quart of cold water, the juice of three oranges; rub the peel of them slightly on sugar, add a glass of Rhine wine, and sweeten at your discretion.

80. Orange Sherbet.

Six ripe, sweet oranges are peeled; four of them cut in pieces and freed from their white skin and seeds, the other two well squeezed.

Stir this with one-fourth pound of sugar over a slow fire to boiling; let it get cool, thin with fresh water, and add the orange pieces, some drops of orange-flower essence, and a few lumps of ice.

81. Turkish Orange Sherbet.

Peel five or six sweet oranges very carefully, divide them into pieces, cut each piece again in two, remove the seeds and the thin skin; put all in a tureen, then place one-fourth pound of powdered sugar and the juice of two oranges in an enameled pot; stir over a slow fire until it begins to boil; take it from the fire, let it get cool, pour it into the tureen, add one quart of cold water, a few drops of orange-flower essence, a few lumps of ice, stir well and serve.

82. Pear Sherbet.

One or two pounds of dried pears are washed, cut in quarters, freed from seeds and pips, infused in one and a half quarts of boiling water in a well-covered tureen over night; the following day add some sugar, stick cinnamon and lemon-peel; boil until the pears are soft, take them out, strain after cooling, add the pears and some lumps of ice, and serve.

(In the same way it may be prepared from fresh pears.)

83. Persian Sherbet.

One pound of ripe, fresh strawberries are mashed in a tureen with a wooden spoon; add a lemon cut in pieces without the seeds, and a teaspoonful of orange-flower water; pour over it one and a fourth quarts of fresh water, let it stand covered three hours.

Strain through canton flannel, press the fruit hard to make them yield as much juice as possible, add one pound of lump-sugar, stir until the sugar is dissolved, put on ice, and serve.

84. Pomegranate Sherbet.

A few ripe pomegranates are cut in pieces; leave some aside, press the rest through a cloth and boil the juice with the same quantity of water and one-fourth pound of sugar, while continually stirring; boil it to a thick syrup.

After it is cool pour it into a tureen, add some fresh water, a few drops of orange-flower water, a few lumps of ice and the fruits you left aside.

85. Turkish Raisin Sherbet.

Boil one pound of fine raisins slowly in one pint of water, until they look like the fresh fruit; filter the fluid, and boil this with one-half pound of sugar to a thick syrup; skim well; let it get cool; pour into a glass bowl; diminish too great a sweetness by adding cold water; put the boiled raisins in, a few drops of orange-flower extract, a few lumps of ice, and serve the sherbet in glasses.

86. Raspberry Lemonade.

Press any quantity of fresh raspberries; add to one quart of juice two quarts of fresh water, the juice of a lemon, and half a pound of powdered sugar; strain, and serve in glasses; or you may bottle it, to keep it for a short while.

87. Rhubarb Sherbet.

Boil as much cut rhubarb as is required for filling half a pint in one quart of water with four ounces of sugar, on which the rind of a small lemon has been rubbed off, for half an hour; strain the water, let the sherbet get cold, add some lumps of ice, and serve this very refreshing drink in glasses.

88. Rose-Hip Lemonade.

Very ripe rose-hips are gathered in the latter part of fall, after the first frost; remove the pits, and let the hips dry in the open air in the sun; for each pint of the dried fruit take two quarts of water; boil both together for half an hour; filter through canton flannel, sweeten to taste with sugar, and serve.

89. Wine Lemonade.

Rub the rind of one and a half lemons on one and a half pounds of loaf-sugar; put it in one quart of cold water and one quart of Rhine wine; add the juice of three lemons; mix well, if desired, with some cracked ice, and serve.

90. Wine Sherbet.

Very ripe raspberries, strawberries, cherries, apricots or peaches, are mashed and infused with water for a few hours; press through a clean cloth; mix the juice with two bottles of white wine, the juice of two lemons, and sugar to taste; place it on ice; after cooling, serve.

91. Catawba Cobbler.

A large, long glass,
> a squirt of Seltzer,
> a barspoonful of sugar; mix this well;
> a wineglassful of Catawba wine; mix this;
> fill your glass with shaved ice to the top,
> 1 dash of port wine.

Ornament with fruits in season.

If you like, put a spoonful of ice-cream on the top, to make it attractive; serve with a straw and a spoon.

92. Champagne Cobbler.

A delicate wineglass,
> a small lump of sugar,
> fill your glass with shaved ice,
> fill the intervals with champagne.

Stir this in a slow manner; add a little vanilla or strawberry ice-cream, with a nice berry in season, and serve with a straw and a spoon. You may add a little maraschino.

93. Sherry Cobbler.

A fine, large glass,
> a spoonful of sugar,
> 1 dash of mineral water; mix this;
> a glass of sherry wine; mix this;
> fill your glass with fine ice,
> a dash of port wine.

Ornament with fruits in season, and ice-cream, and serve with a straw and spoon.

94. Claret Cobbler.

A large, fine glass,
        a squirt of Seltzer,
        a spoonful of sugar; mix this;
        a glass of claret; stir this well;
        fill your glass with fine ice.

Ornament with fruits and ice-cream, and serve with a straw and spoon.

You may add a dash of Jamaica rum before ornamenting.

(These recipes will do for any cobbler you want.)

95. Plain Gin Fizz.

A large mixing-glass,
        the juice of half a lemon or lime,
        ½ spoonful of sugar,
        ⅔ glassful of fine ice,
        a drink of Old Tom or Holland gin.

Shake this exceedingly well; strain into a fizz glass; fill the balance with Seltzer, and see that your guest drinks it at once.

96. Silver Fizz.

It is made in the same way as a plain gin fizz, only begin with the white of an egg in the bottom.

97. Golden Fizz.

It is made the same way as the silver fizz, only begin with the yolk of the egg.

98. Royal Fizz.

It is made the same way as the silver fizz, only begin with the whole of an egg.

99. Grand Royal Fizz.

It is made the same way as the royal fizz, only add a little orange-juice, a dash of maraschino and a dash of parfait amour or crème de roses.

100. Imperial Fizz.

This drink may be prepared, although it is made essentially the same way as the grand royal fizz, out of almost any kind of liquor—such as gin, whiskey or brandy; add, instead of Seltzer or mineral water, champagne. This drink is intended for a company of from three to six persons.

101. Cream Fizz.

This is made the same way as other fizzes, only put a small portion of cream in your glass before shaking; then put in the Seltzer; use a glass a little larger.

102. Violet Fizz.

The juice of half a lemon and half a lime,
  a little sugar in the bottom of a glass,
  ⅔ glassful of fine ice,
  1 drink of Old Tom gin,
  2 dashes of genuine raspberry syrup,
  a pony of cream.
Shake it up quickly, strain into a fizz glass, add a little Seltzer, and serve.

You may use Holland gin instead of Old Tom.

103. Sitting Bull Fizz.

A glass of cracked ice,
  the juice of a large lemon,
  a spoonful of fine sugar,
  ⅓ drink of Santa Cruz rum,
  ⅔ drink of whiskey.
Shake to the freezing-point, strain into a fizz glass and fill the balance with Seltzer.

104. Absinthe Frappé.

(AMERICAN STYLE.)

A mixing-glass with fine ice,
    1 dash of gum,
    1½ ponies of absinthe.

Shake this exceedingly well, strain into a cocktail glass, and serve.

105. Absinthe à la Parisienne.

A medium-sized glass,
    a drink of absinthe in the bottom.

Fill your glass with cold water, by letting it drip into the glass very slowly.

106. Absinthe aux Dieux

A tumbler ⅔ full of ice,
    2 dashes of gum,
    1 pony of absinthe,
    1 dash of maraschino.

Shake it heartily; freeze to the coldest degree; strain into a cocktail glass; drop a little crême de roses in the centre, and serve.

107. The Great Admiral.

(FOR TWO.)

A mixing-tumbler,
    the juice of a peeled orange,
    4 dashes of gum,
    ⅔ glass of fine ice,
    2 dashes of curaçao,
    1 drink of brandy,
    ½ drink of Jamaica rum,
    2 dashes of crême de cocoa,
    1 dash of anisette,
    1 dash of crême de roses.

Mix this very well; strain into fancy glasses, and serve.

108. Alabazam.

A large barglass,
- the juice of ½ lemon,
- 1 barspoonful of sugar,
- 1 dash of Seltzer; mix this well;
- fill your glass ⅔ with fine ice,
- 2 dashes of curaçao,
- 1 drink of brandy.

Stir well, strain, and serve.

109. L'Appetit.

A whiskey-glass,
- 2 lumps of ice,
- ⅔ of vino vermouth,
- ⅓ of Fernet branca,
- 1 slice of orange.

This drink is much *en vogue* among southern Europeans.

110. Apple Blossom.

A glass with ice,
- 4 dashes of gum,
- a small drink of apple-jack,
- 2 dashes of crême de roses.

Freeze this thoroughly; strain, and serve.

111. Après Souper.

(FOR TWO.)

A mixing-glass filled with shaved ice,
- 2 dashes of gum,
- 1 pony of crême de menthe,
- ½ pony of maraschino,
- 1 small drink of brandy.

Stir this, strain and serve.

112. Avant Souper.

A whiskey-tumbler with 2 lumps of ice,
    2 drops of gum,
    1 pony of absinthe.

Let it stand for about two minutes. Fill your glass up with water slowly, by letting the water drip; remove the ice, and serve.

113. Avant Déjeuner.

A large glass with a good portion of imported Seltzer,
    a spoonful of sugar; mix this;
    a glass of Moselle wine; mix this;
    fill up with ice,
    1 dash of port wine.

Ornament the top with fruits in season.

114. L'Arc de Triomphe.

Divide a pint of dry champagne frappé in 2 glasses,
    1 lump of sugar in each with a spoon,
    1 pony of cognac to each glass.

Stir up well before serving.

115. Egg Beer.

Beat a whole egg with a spoonful of sugar in a glass, and fill it up with beer.

116. A Pansy Blossom.

(FOR TWO.)

A large tumbler with some fine ice,
    6 dashes of gum,
    ¼ glass of Russian kümmel,
    ¼ glass of absinthe,
    ¼ glass of vino vermouth,
    ¼ glass of maraschino,
    the whites of two eggs.

Shake to the coldest point; strain into 2 fancy glasses, and serve.

117. Le Bon Boire.

(FOR FOUR.)

A large glass with ice,
- $\frac{1}{10}$ of maraschino,
- $\frac{1}{10}$ of anisette,
- $\frac{1}{10}$ of crême de roses,
- $\frac{1}{10}$ of crême de vanille,
- $\frac{1}{10}$ of parfait amour,
- $\frac{1}{10}$ of crême de thé (tea),
- $\frac{1}{10}$ of celestine,
- $\frac{1}{10}$ of crême de cocoa,
- $\frac{1}{10}$ of fine old brandy,
- $\frac{1}{10}$ of Benedictine.

Shake well, strain, and serve in fancy glasses.

118. Brahmapootra.

An egg, and a spoonful of sugar in a glass,
- a little lemon-juice; fill your glass with ice;
- 1 pony of brandy,
- 1 dash of crême de roses,
- 1 dash of crême de mocha,
- 1 dash of crême de vanille,
- a little cream.

Shake well, strain, and serve.

119. Brandy Crusta.

A mixing-glass,
- a little sugar,
- a little plain water, enough to dissolve it;
- fill the glass $\frac{2}{3}$ full of ice,
- stir this well;
- a drink of brandy; mix again.

Pare a round, clean lemon; place this on the inside of a wine-glass; strain your mixture into it, and serve.

120. Brandy Rose.

A goblet with fine ice,
> 2 dashes of curaçao,
> 2 dashes of parfait amour,
> 1 dash of maraschino,
> ½ dash of peppermint cordial,
> 1 ½ ponies of brandy.

Mix well, and serve.

121. Brandy Toddy.

A mixing-glass,
> half a spoonful of sugar,
> a little water, enough to dissolve the sugar,
> ⅔ full of ice,
> 1 drink of brandy.

Stir this very well; strain into a cocktail glass; grate a little nutmeg on top.

(Any other toddy may be prepared the same way.)

122. The Bridge Bracer.

A large glass with fine ice,
> beat a fresh egg,
> 1 barspoonful of powdered sugar,
> 2 dashes of bitters,
> 1 pony of brandy.

Mix this; add a bottle of imported ginger ale; stir thoroughly, strain, and serve.

123. The Broker's Thought.

The white of an egg in a mixing-glass,
> the juice of a lime,
> a little fine sugar,
> some fine ice,
> ⅔ drink of whiskey,
> ⅓ drink of Santa Cruz rum.

Shake this thoroughly well; strain into a fancy glass; fill up with milk, while you stir it with a spoon, and serve.

124. The Lily Bouquet.

(FOR TWO.)

A goblet with fine ice,
>3 dashes of gum,
>2 ponies of absinthe,
>2 ponies of benedictine,
>2 dashes of crême de roses,
>1 dash of anisette,
>the whites of two eggs.

Shake very well, strain, and serve.

125. Calla Lily.

(FOR TWO.)

In a mixing-glass put the yolks of 2 fresh eggs,
>a spoonful of sugar,
>½ glassful of fine ice,
>1½ ponies of brandy,
>1½ ponies of Jamaica rum,
>1 dash of maraschino,
>2 ponies of cream,
>a few drops of crême de roses;
>shake this well.

Whip the whites of the eggs into a snowy foam with a little sugar. Pour out your drink into two glasses, and crown the whole with the foam.

126. Claret Punch.

A large, thin glass,
>the juice of half a lemon,
>a squirt of Seltzer,
>a spoonful of sugar; mix well;
>a glass of claret; mix this again.

Fill your glass with fine ice to the top; put some ice-cream on top; ornament with orange and berries in season.

127. Chocolate Punch.

A glass with an egg in the bottom,
        a spoonful of sugar,
        ⅔ of brandy,
        ⅓ of port wine,
        1 dash of crême de cocoa,
        1 pony of cream.
Fill your glass with ice; shake well; strain, and serve.

128. Claret Cup.

A good sized bowl,
        ½ pony of maraschino,
        ½ pony of curaçao,
        ½ pony of benedictine,
        ½ pony of chartreuse (yellow),
        the juice of 6 limes,
        2 bottles of claret,
        1 bottle of Rhine wine or Moselle,
        a bottle of Apollinaris,
        ½ pound of sugar,
        a little rind of a cucumber,
        a little orange and pineapple sliced,
        a few sprigs of mint.
Stir this very well; add a little coarse ice, and serve.

129. The Cosmopolitan Cooler.

A long glass,
        the juice of 2 limes,
        a few dashes of Seltzer,
        a spoonful of powdered sugar,
        mix this well;
        a drink of Santa Cruz rum,
        then fill the glass with fine ice,
        stir all ingredients well;
        a dash of Jamaica rum.
Crown it with vanilla ice-cream and ornament with berries lightly powdered with sugar; serve with a straw.

130. Champagne Cup.

It is made like a claret cup, only use champagne instead of claret.

131. Columbus Punch.

The juice of half an orange and the juice of half a lemon in the bottom of the glass; dissolve this with a spoonful of sugar and a dash of mineral water,

    1 glass of Chianti,
    2 dashes of Jamaica rum,
    1 dash of maraschino,
    1 dash of brandy.

Mix this well, fill your glass with fine ice, add a dash of Rosoglio and ornament with fruits and ice-cream.

132. Coffee and Rum.

(FOR COLD AND SORE THROAT.)

Break an egg in a glass, beat it up well;

    a spoonful of sugar,
    a drink of old Jamaica rum.

Mix this up well, pour in a cup of the best mocha or Java coffee—hot—and finish with a piece of best butter. Best take this drink right after rising.

133. The Correspondent.

A pony glass,

    ⅓ of crême de roses,
    ⅓ of green chartreuse,
    ⅓ of brandy.

Light this for two minutes and serve.

134. Easter Crocus.

A large mixing-tumbler,
> a fresh egg in its bottom,
> the juice of ½ a lemon,
> 1 barspoonful of sugar,
> fill the tumbler with ice,
> 1 drink of Old Tom gin,
> 1 dash of maraschino,
> 1 dash of crême de vanille.

Shake this thoroughly well; pour out into a thin glass and fill the little vacant space with ginger ale.

135. The Southern Cross.

A mixing-glass,
> the juice of a lime,
> a dash of mineral water,
> a spoonful of sugar,
> ⅔ of St. Croix rum,
> ⅓ of brandy,
> 1 dash of curaçao.

Stir this well, fill your glass with fine ice, stir again and strain into a sour glass.

136. The Crown.

A pony glass,
> ⅓ of maraschino,
> ⅓ of green chartreuse,
> ⅓ of benedictine, each separate.

137. Curaçao Punch.

A long, thin glass,
> the juice of half a lemon,
> 4 dashes of gum,
> ½ pony of brandy,
> ½ pony of Jamaica rum,
> ½ pony of curaçao.

Fill your glass with ice, stir well, ornament with fruits and ice-cream, serve with a spoon and straw.

138. "The World's" Morning Delight.

A large tumbler,
>the juice of half a lemon,
>the juice of half an orange,
>a little fine sugar,
>2 dashes of Russian kümmel,
>2 dashes of maraschino,
>1½ ponies of absinthe.

Fill your glass with fine ice, shake this well, strain, add some Seltzer and serve.

139. Ladies' Delight.

A large, thin glass,
>a spoonful of sugar,
>a cup of cold coffee,
>⅔ of brandy,
>⅓ of Jamaica rum.

Fill your glass with ice, stir well, ornament with ice-cream and berries, and serve with spoon and a straw.

140. The Duplex.

(FOR TWO.)

Break 2 eggs in a large glass,
>2 barspoonfuls of powdered sugar,
>⅔ full of ice,
>1 drink of sherry,
>1 drink of port wine,
>½ pony of benedictine,
>a small whiskey tumbler of cream.

Shake extremely well and strain into two fine glasses.

141. General Harrison's Egg-Nogg.

It is made as any egg-nogg, only use cider instead of liquor, and no milk.

142. Egg-Nogg.

A large mixing-glass,
>a fresh egg in its bottom,
>a tablespoonful of sugar,
>a little fine ice,
>⅓ of Santa Cruz rum,
>⅔ of brandy,
>1 dash of maraschino or crême de vanille.

Fill your glass with milk; shake this exceedingly well, strain into a large, thin glass, add the oil of a little lemon-peel on the top, and serve.

(This drink may be made of almost any kind of liquor that is desired.)

143. Eye-Opener.

The juice of ½ a lime in a glass,
>a spoonful of sugar,
>the white of an egg,
>a little drink of Irish whiskey,
>2 dashes of Tonic Phospate,
>⅔ full of ice.

Shake, strain and fill balance with Seltzer.

144. The Foundation.

(FOR TWO.)

A large tumbler with 2 fresh eggs,
>the juice of a lemon,
>2 barspoonfuls of sugar,
>½ glass of shaved ice,
>2 dashes of calisaya,
>2 drinks of Old Tom gin,
>1 dash of absinthe,
>2 dashes of vino vermouth.

Shake for full 2 minutes; strain into a high glass; fill the balance with carbonic water, and serve.

145. Encore.

A pony glass,
⅓ of maraschino,
⅓ of curaçao,
⅓ of brandy; each separate.
Light it and serve.

146. Sherry Filler.

The yolk of an egg in a mixing-glass,
a spoonful of sugar,
a drink of sherry wine,
1 dash of crême de roses,
⅔ full of ice.
Shake this well, and serve.

147. Le Fin du Siècle.

(WILLIAM'S PRIDE.)

A mixing-glass with the juice of half an orange,
the juice of ¼ of a lemon,
½ spoonful of sugar,
the yolk of an egg,
½ pony of brandy,
½ pony of benedictine,
½ pony of maraschino,
1 dash of curaçao,
1 dash of anisette,
1 dash of parfait amour,
1 dash of noyeau,
3 ponies of pure cream.

Fill your glass with fine ice, shake it extra well; strain into a fancy glass; ornament the top with the white of an egg, that you have beaten up to the form of frozen snow, and sweetened with sugar; serve with a spoon.

148. Lafayette Flip.

Drop into a large glass a fresh egg,
> 1 barspoonful of powdered sugar,
> 1 pony of old Rye whiskey,
> a dash of green chartreuse,
> 2 dashes of curaçao,
> 2 ponies of cream,
> a few lumps of ice.

Shake this all well, and strain into a fancy glass.

149. Sherry Flip.

(FOR TWO.)

Into a large glass 2 eggs,
> 2 spoonfuls of sugar,
> ¼ glass of fine ice,
> 2 glasses of sherry wine,
> 1 small glass of cream.

Shake this exceedingly well, and serve. You may add a dash of maraschino.

150. Forget-Me-Not.

A mixing-glass with ice,
> the juice of a lime,
> a spoonful of sugar,
> a drink of brandy,
> a dash of maraschino,
> the white of an egg.

Shake this well, strain and serve.

151. Frappé à la Guillaume.

2 dashes of gum in the bottom of the glass,
> fill your glass with ice,
> 1 pony of absinthe,
> ½ pony of vino vermouth,
> 2 dashes of anisette.

Freeze this to the coldest point, and serve.

152. The Mayflower.
(FOR TWO.)

A glass with ice,
> 6 dashes of gum,
> ¼ of Russian kümmel,
> ¼ of brandy,
> ¼ of vino vermouth,
> ¼ of crême de cocoa,
> 1 dash of parfait amour,
> the yolks of two eggs.

Shake well, strain and serve.

153. Fruit Frappé.

Into a mixing-tumbler the juice of half a lemon,
> a little orange-juice,
> 1 barspoonful of sugar,
> 2 barspoonfuls of pineapple syrup,
> 1 pony of rich cream,
> a drink of Santa Cruz rum.

Pack your goblet with fine ice, and shake to the freezing-point; strain into a fancy glass, and serve.

154. Whiskey Frappé.

A large glass with ice,
> 2 dashes of gum,
> a drink of whiskey.

Shake for 2 minutes, and serve.

155. The Judge.

A mixing-glass ⅔ full of ice,
> 3 dashes of gum,
> ⅓ of crême de menthe,
> ⅔ of brandy.

Shake to the freezing-point; strain, and serve in a cocktail glass.

156. Porter Flip.

A long, thin glass with an egg in the bottom,
    a spoonful of sugar,
    fill your glass with porter,
    stir very well.
A little nutmeg on top, and the oil of a little lemon-peel.

157. The Gem.

A mixing-glass,
    the juice of a lime,
    a little pineapple syrup,
    a spoonful of sugar; dissolve well;
    ½ drink of Santa Cruz rum,
    ½ drink of brandy.

Mix this well, fill your glass with ice, and mix again; strain into a fine glass; place a slice of lemon on the top, and grate a little cinnamon upon it.

158. Genuine Whiskey Punch.

A goblet filled with fine ice,
    a dash of lemon-juice,
    3 dashes of gum,
    1 drink of whiskey.

Then fill another goblet with fine ice, and put this on top of the first; turn them upside down five or six times; hold them up together as high as you can with both hands, and let the liquid drip down into a tall, fancy glass; 1 dash of Jamaica rum on the top, and you will have an impressive and pleasant drink.

(Other liquors may be turned into punches the same way.)

159. Gin Puff.

A large glass with a drink of gin; fill your glass half with milk and the balance with Seltzer, while you stir it.

160. Gilmore Punch.

The juice of a lime in a fine, tall glass,
> the juice of half an orange,
> a small spoonful of sugar; mix this;
> fill the glass with cracked ice,
> 1 dash of maraschino,
> 1 dash of curaçao,
> 1 dash of green chartreuse,
> 1 dash of benedictine,
> 1 drink of Irish whiskey.

Stir well, and ornament with vanilla ice-cream and fruits in season.

161. The Glorious Fourth.

A glass with the juice of a lime,
> 4 dashes of gum,
> ⅔ full of ice,
> 1 drink of brandy,
> 1 dash of Jamaica rum,
> a large tablespoonful of ice-cream.

Shake this exceedingly well; strain into a fancy glass, and serve.

162. Hannibal Hamlin.

A mixing-tumbler,
> the juice of half a lemon,
> the juice of half an orange,
> fill it with cracked ice,
> ⅔ of peach brandy,
> ⅓ of old Jamaica rum,
> 2 tablespoonfuls of honey.

Shake to the freezing-point, and strain into a fancy glass.

163. Happy Moment.

A pony glass,
> ⅓ of crême de roses,
> ⅓ of maraschino,
> ⅓ of benedictine,
> 1 drop of bitters in the centre.

164. Heart's Content.
(FOR TWO.)

A mixing-glass with ⅔ of fine ice,
  1 pony of brandy,
  1 pony of benedictine,
  1 pony of maraschino,
  1 pony of parfait amour.

Shake this thoroughly; strain into fine wineglasses; beat up the white of an egg to the form of frozen snow with a little sugar; put this on top of your drink; squeeze a little lemon-peel on it, and serve with a spoon.

165. My Hope.

A whiskey glass with 2 dashes of gum,
  1 dash of bitters,
  ⅔ of brandy,
  ⅓ of port wine,
  a little red pepper.

Stir this well, and serve.

166. The Invitation.
(FOR TWO.)

A glass with 2 dashes of gum,
  some fine ice,
  1 small drink of sherry wine,
  1 small drink of vino vermouth,
  2 dashes of absinthe.

Freeze this to the coldest point; strain into 2 fancy glasses, and serve.

167. Jamaica Rum à la Créole.

The juice of half a lime,
  a dash of Seltzer,
  1 spoonful of sugar; dissolve this;
  a drink of Jamaica rum; mix this;
  fill your glass with ice,
  a dash of port wine.

Ornament with fruits and ice-cream.

168. John Collins.

A large glass with the juice of half a lemon,
        a spoonful of sugar,
        a full drink of Holland gin.
Mix this well; add two or three lumps of ice; fill your glass up with Seltzer, while you stir.

169. The Kaleidoscope.

A mixing-glass with some cracked ice,
        1 pony of absinthe,
        1 pony of vino vermouth,
        3 dashes of maraschino,
        3 dashes of benedictine,
        3 dashes of curaçao,
        3 dashes of crême de cocoa.
Shake to the freezing-point; strain into a fine wineglass, and serve.

170. The Knickerbocker.

The juice of half a lime or lemon in a glass,
        3 dashes of raspberry syrup,
        1 wineglassful of Jamaica rum,
        1 dash of curaçao,
        a little cracked ice.
Stir this well; strain, and serve in a fancy glass.

171. The Ladies' Great Favorite.

A large glass,
        a squirt of Seltzer,
        a spoonful of fine sugar,
        fill a wineglass half full with sherry and
        the other half with port wine,
        1 dash of brandy;
        mix this well.
Fill your glass with shaved ice; ornament with orange and pineapple, and top it off with ice-cream; serve with a spoon.

172. Lait de Poule.

(FOR LADIES.)

Beat the yolk of an egg with 2 tablespoonfuls of powdered sugar to foam,

> a pony of rum, or kirschwasser, etc.

Stir continually while filling the glass with hot milk, and serve.

173. A Maiden's Kiss.

> $\frac{1}{5}$ of maraschino in a sherry glass,
> $\frac{1}{5}$ of crême de roses,
> $\frac{1}{5}$ of curaçao (white),
> $\frac{1}{5}$ of chartreuse (yellow),
> $\frac{1}{5}$ of benedictine, each separate.

174. The Manhattan Cooler.

A large glass,

> the juice of a lime,
> a spoonful of sugar; mix this well;
> 3 or 4 lumps of ice,
> 1 glass of claret,
> 1 dash of Santa Cruz rum,
> 1 bottle of plain soda.

Mix this and serve with a little fruit.

175. The Mayor.

(AN IMITATION OF A MINT JULEP.)

A large glass with an egg in the bottom,

> a barspoonful of sugar,
> 2 dashes of absinthe,
> $\frac{1}{3}$ of vino vermouth,
> $\frac{2}{3}$ of kümmel,
> 2 gills of cream.

Fill your glass with ice; freeze to the lowest point; strain into a tall glass; squeeze a little lemon-peel on it.

176. Our Milk Punch.

A large glass,
> ⅔ of Santa Cruz rum,
> ⅓ of brandy,
> 1 dash of crême de vanille,
> 1 spoonful of sugar,
> a little fine ice.

Fill your glass with milk, shake thoroughly, strain and serve,
Add a little nutmeg, if you wish, or squeeze a little lemon-peel on it.

177. Strained Mint Julep.

Put the leaves of two sprigs of mint in a mixing-glass with a spoonful of sugar and a little water to dissolve it.

With a squeezing-stick squeeze out the extract of the leaves,
> 1 drink of brandy.

Fill your glass with ice; stir well, strain into a long champagne glass, add a dash of Jamaica rum on the top carefully; place a little sprig of mint on the side of the glass, sprinkle a little sugar on the leaves, and serve.

(You may use other liquors instead of brandy.)

178. Mint Julep.

Use a large, long glass; select three long sprigs of luxuriant mint and let the stems rest on the bottom of the glass. Then take two sprigs of mint, strip them and put the leaves in a mixing-glass; 1 spoonful of sugar, 1 squirt of Seltzer; crush out the extract of the leaves with a squeezing-stick; 1 drink of brandy; stir this and strain into your original glass; fill it with ice and stir; a dash of Jamaica rum on top, ornament the brim of the glass with fruits and the centre with ice-cream and berries. Sprinkle a little sugar over your leaves and serve with a straw.

You may put a little rosebud on your drink.

179. The Ne Plus Ultra.

A sherry glass,
> ¼ of crême de roses,
> ¼ of green chartreuse,
> ¼ of benedictine,
> ¼ of brandy.

Set fire to the brandy, let burn for two minutes, and serve.

180. The Morning Delight.

In a mixing-glass put the white of an egg,
> the juice of a lime,
> the juice of half an orange,
> fill your glass with ice,
> ½ pony of absinthe,
> 1 pony of whiskey,
> ½ pony of sherry wine,
> 1 spoonful of sugar,
> 2 dashes of calisaya.

Shake this well; strain into a fancy glass and fill the balance with seltzer.

181. The Nap.

A cocktail glass filled with ice,
> ⅓ of kümmel,
> ⅓ of green chartreuse,
> ⅓ of brandy.

Drop a dash of crême de roses on top, which will go to the bottom, and serve.

182. New Orleans Punch.

A thin glass with the juice of half a lemon,
> 1 spoonful of sugar; mix this;
> fill with fine ice,
> ⅔ of St. Julien,
> ⅓ of Jamaica rum,
> 1 dash of brandy.

Stir this very well; ornament with fruits in season and a little ice-cream on the top, and serve with a straw.

183. The Opera.

(FOR TWO.)

Break two eggs in the bottom of a mixing-glass,
2 barspoonfuls of powdered sugar,
2 ponies of fine brandy,
fill your glass with cracked ice.

Shake the mixture thoroughly.

A pint bottle of champagne as cold as possible is poured out into two ice-cold glasses with room enough for your first mixture, which is to be strained into the cold champagne very slowly; care must be taken not to have the mixture overflow.

184. Orange County Pride.

A goblet with the juice of a lime,
a squirt of Seltzer,
a spoonful of sugar; dissolve this well;
1 drink of apple-jack.

Fill your glass with ice to the top and stir. Add a dash of dark-colored brandy; ornament with fruits and serve with a straw.

185. Orange County Punch.

A mixing-glass with a fresh egg in the bottom,
the juice of a lemon,
1 barspoonful of powdered sugar,
a glass of fine apple cider,
fill with ice.

Shake thoroughly, strain, and fill up with Seltzer.

186. Palate Tickler.

(FOR COLD.)

A little lemon-juice in a tumbler with some genuine New Orleans molasses,
a drink of old Jamaica rum.

Stir exceedingly well, and serve.

187. The "New York Herald."

(FOR TWO.)

A large mixing-glass with the yolks of two eggs in the bottom,
        the juice of an orange,
        a little pineapple juice,
        1 barspoonful of sugar,
        1 drink of fine brandy,
        1 pony of kirschwasser,
        ½ pony of curaçao,
        ½ pony of maraschino,
        ½ pony of crême de roses,
        2 dashes of benedictine,
        2 dashes of crême de cocoa.

Fill your glass with fine ice; a large claret glass with pure cream; shake this exceedingly well; strain into two fancy glasses so as to fill them. Beat up the white of one egg to the form of frozen snow; sweeten this well with sugar; put this on the top of your drinks; squeeze a little lemon-peel on each, and serve with a spoon. This is intended for an evening drink, only on special occasions.

188. The Paymaster.

A cocktail glass with fine ice,
        ⅔ of crême de menthe,
        ⅓ of brandy.

Drop a little bitters in the centre and put a piece of lemon-peel on the brim of the glass; serve.

189. Peach and Honey.

A whiskey tumbler,
        the juice of half a lime or lemon,
        a good part of real honey,
        a drink of peach brandy.

Stir very well before serving.
(Molasses may be used; also Jamaica rum.)

190. Piazza.

(A VARIATION OF THE OLD FLOSTER.)

A barspoonful of sugar in a large glass,
   a bottle of plain soda,
   2 or 3 lumps of ice,
   a drink of sherry,
   a dash of crême de cocoa.

Mix this thoroughly well, and serve.
This is a drink specially delicious when you are thirsty.

191. Pineapple Julep.

A large glass, with a little pineapple-juice,
   the juice of one-fourth of an orange,
   2 dashes of raspberry syrup,
   2 dashes of maraschino,
   ½ pony of old gin,
   1 glass of champagne or sparkling wine.

Fill your glass with ice, stir this very well, ornament with fruits and ice-cream, and serve with a straw.

192. Pineapple Punch.

A large glass,
   ½ wineglassful of pineapple-juice,
   the juice of half an orange,
   2 dashes of raspberry syrup,
   a little sugar,
   1 dash of maraschino,
   ½ drink of Tom gin,
   ½ drink of Moselle wine.

Stir well; fill your glass with ice; ornament with pineapple and berries, and serve with a straw.

193. The Poem.

A pony glass,
   ⅓ of crême de roses,
   ⅓ of curaçao,
   ⅓ of benedictine, each separate.

194. Porter Sangaree.

A long, thin glass,
        a spoonful of sugar,
        fill your glass with porter.

Stir very well, add a little nutmeg and squeeze a little lemon-peel on top.

195. Port-Wine Sangaree.

A mixing-glass with fine ice,
        3 dashes of gum,
        1 glass of port wine.

Stir this very well, strain into a fine, tall glass, cut a few slices of a peeled lemon, drop them in the drink, grate a little nutmeg on the top and present.

(Other sangarees may be prepared the same way.)

196. The Primrose.

A long, thin glass,
        the juice of half an orange,
        ½ spoonful of sugar,
        1 dash of mineral water,
        1 dash of parfait amour,
        ⅔ of sherry wine,
        ⅓ of port wine.

Mix this well; fill your glass with ice; ornament with fruits and ice-cream.

197. The Press.

The white of an egg in the bottom of a glass,
        3 dashes of lemon-juice,
        1 spoonful of sugar,
        ⅔ of whiskey,
        1 dash of St. Croix rum,
        1 dash of calisaya,
        1 dash of absinthe.

Fill your glass with ice, shake well, strain into a fizz-glass, and fill the balance with Seltzer.

198. Pousse l' Amour.

Fill a sherry glass,
> ⅓ of maraschino,
> the yolk of one fresh egg,
> ⅓ of crême de roses,
> ⅓ of brandy, each separate.

199. The Promenade.

An egg in the bottom of the glass,
> the glass two-thirds full of fine ice,
> a barspoonful of fine sugar,
> ⅔ pony of brandy,
> ⅓ pony of crême de cocoa,
> ½ pony of port wine,
> 2 ponies of cream,

Shake this very well, and strain into a fancy glass.

200. Pousse Café.

A sherry glass,
> ⅙ of crême de roses, or raspberry syrup,
> ⅙ of maraschino,
> ⅙ of curaçao,
> ⅙ of benedictine,
> ⅙ of chartreuse (green),
> ⅙ of brandy, each separate.

You may drop in a little bitters on the top, and set fire to the brandy. While burning, squeeze a little orange-peel on it, which will produce a fine pyrotechnical effect.)

201. The "World's" Pousse Café.

> ¼ of maraschino,
> ¼ of crême de roses,
> ¼ of benedictine,
> ¼ of brandy, each separate.

A drop of bitters in the centre; set fire to the brandy, and serve.

202. La Première.

(FOR TWO.)

Place the leaves of four sprigs of mint and one-half spoonful of sugar in a large tumbler,
    2 dashes of mineral water.

Squeeze out the extract, to give it a dark green tincture. Fill your tumbler two-thirds full of chopped ice; add two small drinks of Tom gin; stir to a very cold degree; strain into two cocktail glasses; place a small sprig of mint in each, allowing the stem to rest on the bottom; sprinkle a little sugar on the leaves; add a little champagne, and serve.

203. The Life-Prolonger.

A large glass, with a fresh egg,
    1 spoonful of fine sugar,
    ⅔ full of fine ice,
    ⅔ of sherry wine,
    ⅓ of port wine,
    1 dash of crême de roses,
    2 ponies of cream.

Shake this exceedingly well, strain into a large glass, and serve.

204. The Queen of Night.

A glass, with a dash of chartreuse in the bottom,
    ⅔ of port wine,
    ⅓ of Madeira,
    1 dash of brandy,
    1 dash of crême de roses,
    2 dashes of gum.

Fill your glass with ice; mix well; strain, and serve in a cut glass.

205. The Queen of Sheba.

(FOR TWO.)

A large glass, with the yolks of two eggs,
- 2 barspoonfuls of sugar,
- 1 dash of vino vermouth,
- 1 dash of port wine,
- 2 dashes of sherry,
- 1½ drinks of brandy,
- 2 dashes of maraschino,
- 1 dash of curaçao.

Fill your glass with ice; shake well, strain into two long, thin glasses; crown them with the whites of the two eggs beaten to a hard consistency, and sprinkle colored sugar on the top of it.

206. The Rainbow.

A sherry glass,
- ⅐ of maraschino,
- ⅐ of crême de menthe,
- ⅐ of apricotine,
- ⅐ of curaçao,
- ⅐ of yellow chartreuse,
- ⅐ of green chartreuse,
- ⅐ of brandy, each separate.

Set fire to the brandy, and serve.

207. The Reliever.

The white of an egg in the bottom of a glass,
- the juice of half a lemon,
- a barspoonful of sugar,
- ⅔ glass of fine ice,
- ⅔ of Jamaica rum,
- ⅓ of port wine.

Shake this for a full minute; strain into a fancy glass, and serve.

208. The Reminder.

A goblet, with
- 1 dash of maraschino,
- 1 dash of crême de roses,
- ⅔ glass of fine ice,
- ⅓ of sherry,
- ⅓ of port wine,
- ⅓ of vino vermouth.

Mix this thoroughly; strain into a fancy glass, and serve.

209. Roman Punch.

A large, thin glass,
- the juice of an orange,
- the juice of half a lime or lemon in the bottom,
- a spoonful of sugar,
- a squirt of mineral water,
- dissolve this well;
- ½ pony of curaçao,
- ½ pony of maraschino,
- 1 pony of brandy,
- 1 dash of Jamaica rum.

Mix this thoroughly well; fill your glass with fine ice; ornament the brim with oranges and pineapple, and the centre with ice-cream and berries. Serve with a spoon and a straw.

210. Reverie.

A mixing-glass, with ice,
- 2 dashes of gum,
- 1 pony of brandy,
- ½ pony of maraschino,
- ½ pony of curaçao,
- ⅓ glass of vanilla ice-cream.

Shake this very well; strain and serve.

211. The Requiem.

In a mixing-glass an egg,
>a spoonful of powdered sugar,
>1 pony of brandy,
>1 dash of sherry,
>1 dash of port wine,
>1 dash of maraschino,
>1 pony of cream.

Fill your glass with ice, shake it and strain into a high champagne glass.

212. Sans Souci.

(FOR TWO.)

A large glass, with the juice of a lime or lemon,
>a spoonful of sugar,
>the yolks of two eggs,
>fill your glass two-thirds full of ice,
>2 ponies of absinthe,
>1 pony of maraschino,
>1 pony of vermouth,
>1 dash of white curaçao.

Shake this exceedingly well; strain into two fancy wine-glasses, beat up the white of one egg to the form of frozen snow, with some sugar; put this on top of your two drinks, and serve with a spoon.

213. The Senator.

A glass with shaved ice,
>⅙ of brandy,
>⅙ of maraschino,
>⅙ of curaçao,
>⅙ of chartreuse,
>⅙ of benedictine,
>⅙ of crême de roses.

Shake this well, strain into a cocktail glass, and serve.

214. The Shandy Gaff.

A glass of Bass ale and a glass of ginger ale are mixed in a glass together, and served.

215. The Snowball.

A large glass with an egg; beat up well with a little powdered sugar, add a bottle of genuine cold ginger ale while you stir it thoroughly, and serve. You may add a pony of brandy.

216. "The Sun."

The juice of half an orange and half a lime in the bottom of a large, thin glass; add and dissolve a spoonful of powdered sugar with a dash of mineral water,

    1 pony of fine brandy,
    ½ pony of Jamaica rum,
    1 dash of benedictine,
    1 dash of curaçao,
    1 dash of crême de roses.

Mix this thoroughly, fill your glass with fine ice; stir well; ornament with frozen snow in the centre, and the brim with fruits; write on the top of the snow "The Sun," with nutmeg.

Should you have no real snow, beat up the white of an egg with a little fine sugar.

217. "The Evening Sun."

(FOR FOUR.)

In a large glass,

    the juice of a large lemon,
    2 barspoonfuls of powdered sugar,
    fill the glass with chopped ice,
    a drink of fine brandy,
    a pony of green chartreuse,
    ½ pony of crême de roses,
    the whites of 2 eggs.

Shake this to the freezing-point.

In four glasses divide a pint of dry champagne; strain your ingredients into these four glasses very slowly, and serve.

218. Tansy and Gin.

Place a little tansy in a tumbler, add a little sugar, mix with a little water to extract the substance of the tansy; pour in gin (Holland or Old Tom), and serve with a spoon.

219. Tom and Jerry.

Break the yolks of six eggs in the bottom of a large bowl; beat it long enough to make bubbles appear on the top; stir in some fine sugar gradually, until the mixture becomes hard enough, so that you may take out a spoonful of it without spilling anything; beat the whites of the eggs into the form of frozen snow in another bowl; add one-half of this to your first mixture; mix this together with two ponies of maraschino and two ponies of crême de vanille, take a tablespoonful of this mixture in a fancy Tom-and-Jerry cup; add a small drink of either brandy, whiskey, rum, sherry wine or port wine; mix this well; fill the balance with boiling milk; put a little of the white of the eggs you have got left on the top; add a little ground cinnamon and your drink is ready.

(To keep your mixture in the bowl from getting hard, put a small glass of ale on the top.)

220. Tip-Top Sip.

A goblet with a dash of crême de roses,
> 1 dash of absinthe,
> ⅓ of sherry wine,
> ⅓ of port wine,
> ⅓ of vino vermouth,
> a little fine ice.

Mix this thoroughly, strain into a fancy glass, and present.

221. La Vie Parisienne.

Mix one part of Burgundy and two parts of champagne in your glass. (This drink is one of the richest.)

Also porter (Dublin Stout) may be mixed the same way with champagne with a most satisfactory result.

222. Tom Collins.

The juice of half a lemon in a large glass,
        a barspoonful of sugar,
        a drink of Tom gin; mix this well;
        2 lumps of ice,
        a bottle of plain soda.
Mix well and serve.

223. Bunch of Violets.

(FOR TWO.)

Put an egg in a mixing-glass,
        a spoonful of sugar,
        $\frac{1}{6}$ of benedictine,
        $\frac{1}{6}$ of maraschino,
        $\frac{1}{6}$ of anisette,
        $\frac{1}{6}$ of vino vermouth,
        $\frac{1}{6}$ of crême de vanille,
        $\frac{1}{6}$ of chartreuse,
        2 ponies of cream.

Fill your glass with ice; freeze into a jelly, and strain into long glasses, and serve.

224. William's Summer Cooler.

In a very long cut glass the juice of two limes,
        a spoonful of powdered sugar,
        a good dash of Seltzer; dissolve this well;
        1 pony of Santa Cruz rum,
        1 glass of California claret; mix this.

Fill your glass with ice; ornament with slices of orange and pineapple, and ice-cream, and top off with strawberries or other berries in season.

225. Whiskey Sling.

A goblet with a little fine ice,
        2 dashes of gum,
        1 drink of whiskey.
Stir this well, strain and serve.

Medical Drinks.

226.

A handful of fresh tansy is infused in a bottle of gin, this being the best, although other liquors may be used, too; infuse for twenty-four hours at least. One-third of a drink will be sufficient for a drink, and be a good appetizer.

227.

About a dozen fresh stalks of calamus are infused in a bottle of gin for twenty-four hours and served like the former. It is excellent for cramps.

Liquors and Ratafias.

Introduction to Liquors and Ratafias.

THE manufacture of these alcoholic beverages is done, firstly, by distillation, by which method the finest liquors are obtained; secondly, by extraction, and thirdly, by simply mixing volatile extracts of plants to cognac spirits, etc. They all contain larger or smaller quantities of dissolved sugar, and various aromatic or spicy ingredients.

Distillation is more complicated and troublesome than the two other methods, but it secures products of far higher fineness and value; yet the requirement of the apparatus necessary for manufacturing them renders the application too difficult in a household; furthermore, a profound knowledge of chemistry, great practice and dexterity are required; therefore, this manufacturing is better left to large establishments. The best and most exquisite liquors of this kind are imported from Dantzic, Breslau, Berlin, Stettin, Hamburg, Mannheim, Vienna, Trieste, Amsterdam, Italy, Bordeaux, Paris, and the West Indies. The recipes to manufacture the most famous among them are mostly kept secret; moreover, the foreign ratafias may not easily be imitated because many of the herbs and fruits required for the purpose are not growing in this country.

LIQUORS AND RATAFIAS.

To prepare good and very palatable liquors for the family use we put down a series of recipes, as verified by our own experience, and that of others. But we declare here candidly and freely, that it is absolutely impossible to obtain by extraction the same liquors as by distillation. The liquors won by infusing fruits or blossoms, or by mixing with fruit-juices are called ratafias; the fine French, very sweet, and, on account of this, more consistent liquors are called crêmes or huiles (oils): *crême de vanille, crême de Barbados, crême de café, de canelle, de chocolat, huile de rose, huile de Venus, de Jupiter, de Cythère, des demoiselles,* etc.

228. Absinthe.

A strong liquor made of vermouth; it is mainly drunk in France; it is said to strengthen the stomach. Swiss absinthe is the most renowned one.

Recipe: To four quarts of cognac spirits take eight ounces of anise, one ounce of star anise, four ounces of great and four ounces of small fennel, one ounce of coriander, one-fourth ounce of angelica root, one ounce of angel sweet root, half an ounce of licorice, half an ounce of calamus, half an ounce of bitter almonds, one ounce of great and one ounce of small leaves of vermouth, one-fourth ounce of peppermint leaves, half an ounce of camilles, one-fourth ounce of juniper; let all these ingredients distill from three to four weeks on a warm place, or in the sunlight; filter and fill into bottles.

229. Almonds' Essence.

One and a half pounds of sweet and four ounces of bitter almonds are poured over with boiling water in a sieve; skin and dry them; grind them very fine by adding from one to one and a half pints of cold water.

Refine three pounds of sugar to what is called *sucre à la plume*, *i.e.*, boil the sugar in water until the sugar, sticking to the wooden spoon can be blown off in bubbles of the size of a pea; add now the ground almonds; let all boil up once, and cool off well covered; press through a hair sieve, fill into small bottles, cork well, and keep them on a cool place.

230. Ananas Cordial.

Cut one-fourth of an unpeeled pineapple into small pieces; boil one quart of water with six ounces of lump-sugar; skin carefully; add the pineapple, and put all in a great stone jar or a demijohn; pour three pints of old Jamaica rum or brandy over it; let it soak a fortnight on a warm place; filter and fill into bottles.

231. Angelica Cordial.

Cut one ounce of fresh or dried angelica into small pieces, put it with one-sixth ounce of cloves, one-sixth ounce of cardamom, one-third ounce of stick cinnamon in a demijohn; pour over it three pints of cognac; let it stand about four weeks in a warm place: sweeten with one pound of lump-sugar refined and cleared in one pint of boiling water.

232. Anisette Cordial.

A fine French cordial; the best one comes from Bordeaux; it is to be warmly recommended after rich dinners, as it helps digestion.

Take six quarts of cognac, four ounces of pulverized star anise, four ounces of ordinary anise, the peel of two lemons, one ounce of stick cinnamon; let this stand four weeks in the sun, or in a warm place; sweeten with two and a half pounds of lump-sugar, refined and cleared in three quarts of boiling water; filter and bottle.

233. Apricot Cordial.

Twenty-five apricots are cut in two; mash their pits, and put all in a stone jar; add half a pound of sugar, six cloves, and half a stick of cinnamon; pour one quart of cognac over it, cover or cork it well; let it stand about three weeks in a warm place, shake it once in a while; filter, and bottle.

234. Arrack.

Arrack is a strong, alcoholic beverage of light yellow color; it is prepared in the East and West Indies from the juice of the areca palm-tree, from the sugary juice of the blossoms of the cocoa palm-tree, which is called toddy, from sugar-molasses or from rice with palm-juice.

The arrack of Goa and Batavia are the best brands and of very delicious odor and taste. The manufacturing is mostly done in very simple, imperfect apparatus, chiefly on Java: the best brand there is called Kiji, the second, Taupo, the last, Sichow.

235. Balm Cordial.

Infuse in one quart of fine cognac a handful of balm-leaves for twenty-four hours in the sunlight or upon the stove; remove the leaves, add one pound of powdered sugar, expose the cordial two days to the sun, until the sugar is all dissolved; filter, and bottle.

236. Basle Kirschwasser.

This well-known, famous liquor is obtained in Switzerland, mainly in the vicinity of Basle and in the Black Forest from the black and very sweet berries of the wood-cherries; gather them when they are very ripe in dry weather; free them from their stalks, and mash them in large tubs with wooden mashers; mash also a part of the pits; then fill the entire substance into casks, each two-thirds full, and cover the bunghole.

The fermentation begins soon, and lasts nearly three weeks; after fermentation is done, bring the whole into a distilling apparatus; continue distilling while slowly heating, until absolutely light, colorless kirschwasser is distilled over to the condenser. This distillate is distilled over again, and filled into bottles.

Many trials have been made to find an equivalent for this excellent cordial, but in vain; never take any but the genuine imported Basle kirschwasser.

237. Bilberry Cordial.

Infuse any quantity of red bilberries in a wide-necked, large bottle with enough cognac to cover them; cork the bottle, place it on a sunny spot, and let it stand until the berries have lost their red color. Filter, add to each quart of liquor one pound of refined sugar-syrup, and bottle.

It is a favorite drink in Sweden and Russia.

238. Benedictine.

The active part of the genuine Benedictine cordial is composed nearly exclusively of plants growing on the steep precipices of Normandy; they are gathered and infused at the time when the sap rises, and the blossoms spring forth. These herbs, growing near the sea, are saturated with bromine, iodine, and chloruret of sodium, and develop and keep their healing power in the alcoholic liquids; only best cognac is used for infusion.

239. Bishop Cordial.

Peel twelve bitter oranges, infuse the rind with one quart of old Jamaica rum or arrack de Batavia in a well-covered tureen for twenty-four hours; strain the fluid, and fill it into small bottles, cork, and seal.

Use two tablespoonfuls of this essence to a bottle of claret, and sweeten to taste.

240. Bitter-Orange Cordial.

Put the rind of six thinly peeled bitter oranges in a stone pot, add the filtered juice of the fruit and two quarts of best brandy;

let it soak for three days, well covered; clear and refine one and a half pounds of sugar, add it to the liquor, filter and bottle; do not use it before six months.

241. Another.

Make with a fine needle little holes in the skin of six bitter oranges, place them in a large bottle; pour in two and a half quarts of brandy; let soak for four weeks, add syrup made of one and a half pounds of sugar and one pint of water; filter and bottle.

242. Cassis Liqueur.

Put one pint of mashed black currants in a big bottle; add half a pound of pulverized sugar and one quart of cognac; cork the bottle well, and let it stand for six weeks in the sun; shake daily; then strain through canton flannel, bottle, and let the bottles lie for a while.

243. Cassis Ratafia.

Put in a stone pot one quart of well-cleaned black currants; mash them, add twenty to thirty raspberries, tied up with some cloves in a little muslin bag; add two and a half quarts of brandy; let it stand for eight weeks; filter; mix it with one pound of sugar refined to syrup, which must be still hot; let it again stand for some days, then filter, and bottle.

244. Chartreuse.

The preparation of this famous cordial and its trade is monopolized by the monks of the monastery Grande Chartreuse, in the French département Isère; the monastery was built by St. Bruno in the year 1086.

The monks keep their secret very carefully; an imitation may be obtained in the following way: Take one pint of the best brandy or kirschwasser, eight drops of vermouth essence, one drop of cinnamon essence, one drop of rose essence, and twelve ounces of sugar that was refined and cleared in one pint of water; strain through flannel, cork, seal, and let it lie at least eight weeks.

245. Cherry Cordial à la Française.

A sufficient quantity, half of sweet and half of sour cherries, is cleaned and mashed; press the juice through a hair-sieve so as to receive two quarts of juice, which is to be poured into a tureen; add one quart of currant-juice, two pounds of powdered sugar, the pits washed and cracked; stir the mixture now and then in order to dissolve the sugar; after this add four quarts of brandy, let soak six days in the well-covered tureen, filter, and bottle.

246. Another.

Put a quantity of very ripe, partly mashed, sour cherries in a tureen; add one-sixth of their weight of ripe, likewise partly mashed raspberries, and a handful of cracked cherry-pits; let it stand a week, then filter the juice; add to each three quarts as much cognac; fill the liquor into a large glass jar; shake often; expose it to the sun for four weeks, filter again, and bottle.

247. English Cherry Brandy.

Twenty pounds of wild cherries are freed of their pits; the pits are pulverized, and with the cherries infused in ten quarts of brandy in a covered stone jar for six weeks; add four pounds of refined sugar, filter, and bottle, but use only after a few months.

248. Another.

Six pounds of wild cherries, six pounds of Armenian cherries, and two pounds of raspberries are mashed and put in a small cask; add three pounds of sugar, twelve cloves, half an ounce of powdered cinnamon, one grated nutmeg, a handful of mint leaves, and seven quarts of fine brandy or gin; bung after ten days, and bottle the brandy after two months.

249. Cherry Ratafia.

For the manufacture of a good and palatable cherry ratafia without a distilling apparatus, we add a couple of recipes:

Fill one and a fourth quarts of brandy, one pound of pulverized sugar, one pound of pulverized sweet and one pound of pulverized sour cherries, half a pint of black currants, one-tenth ounce of cinnamon into a large bottle; expose for three days to the sunlight; filter, bottle, and use after a few weeks.

250. Another.

Eight pounds of sour cherries are freed from their pits, and all are put in a stone pot; add one pound of raspberries, half a pound of currants, one and a half ounces of pulverized almonds, one-fourth ounce of cloves, one-half ounce of powdered cinnamon, one-half ounce of mace; infuse this in four quarts of cognac in a covered pot, for three weeks, on a place that is equally warm; shake daily once, add three pounds of cleared and refined sugar; filter and bottle.

251. Another.

Mash two pounds of sour cherries, put them in a wide-necked bottle, add one quart of cognac, cork well, and let it stand for four weeks.

252. Christophlet.

Grate three-fourths of an ounce of cinnamon, three-fourths ounce of cloves, three-fourths ounce of cardamom, three-fourths ounce of cubebs; put this with one pound of lump-sugar in three pints of claret; cover it well, and let it slowly boil; after cooling add one and a fourth quarts of brandy; strain through canton flannel, bottle, cork, seal, and keep in a dry place.

253. Cinnamon Cordial.

Boil one-fourth pound of roughly pulverized Ceylon cinnamon in one quart of water, half an hour; add one and a half pounds of sugar, and refine it in the cinnamon water; after getting cool mix with one and a half quarts of brandy; cork well, let stand for a few days in a warm place, filter and bottle.

254. Clove Cordial.

Infuse in a big glass jar one-fourth ounce of roughly pulverized cloves, half an ounce of likewise prepared coriander, and a handful of dried cherries in a quart of brandy, five weeks, in the sun or on a warm place; shake daily. Clear and refine five ounces of sugar in half a pint of water; skim very carefully, let it get a little cool, add the infusion and filter through blotting-paper and glass funnel; bottle and let it lie for a few weeks.

255. Coffee Liqueur.

Roast three ounces of the best mocha; grind it; prepare a syrup out of one pound of sugar and half a pound of water; put the coffee in the boiling syrup, and let it boil for a few seconds; mix all with one quart of brandy, cork well, and let it stand for a month; then filter, and the liquor is ready for use.

256. Cognac.

All liquors obtained by distillation of the grape-juice are usually called cognac in France, although only that prepared in the city of Cognac, in the arrondissement of the département Charente, deserves this name; this is the best, while those from Languedoc, Armagnac, Auris, Rochelle, and Bordeaux, are all of inferior quality and less aromatic; but even in the genuine cognac we have to distinguish between many different brands, which depend upon its age, and the results of the wine crop. In France it also has the names "*Trois-six*," corresponding to its percentage of alcohol, and "*Eau de vie*," while the English call it "brandy." Charente and Gironde alone produce yearly more than one million hektoliters (1 hektoliter=105.67 liquid quarts). The fineness of this liquor increases with its age, and when old enough, assumes the taste of an exceedingly fine, spirituous wine. There are many imitations, mostly with spirits of 90° proof, cognac oil and coloring.

257. Curaçao.

This famous liquor is manufactured best in Amsterdam by infusing curaçao peel in very good brandy that has been sweetened with sugar syrup. The curaçao fruit is a species of the bitter orange, that grows mainly in Curaçao, one of the Lesser Antilles, north of Venezuela, and the greatest Dutch colony in the West Indies.

258. Currant Ratafia.

Fill into a large stone pot or jar four quarts of good brandy, two quarts of currant-juice—you obtain this juice by placing the pot with the currants within a larger vessel partly filled with water, which is heated until the currants in the smaller pot burst—add three pounds of sugar, a stick of cinnamon, some cloves; let it stand four weeks; stir daily; filter through flannel, and bottle.

259. Currant Metheglin.

The juice of eight quarts of currants is mixed with twenty quarts of boiling water in which eight pounds of honey are dissolved; add one ounce of cremor tartari; stir well for a quarter of an hour; when the fermentation is over and the liquid is clear, add one quart of brandy; bottle at once, fasten the corks with wire, and place the bottles in the cellar; you may use the beverage after six weeks.

260. English Elder Brandy.

Squeeze the juice of a large quantity of elderberries through a cloth; boil up with sugar and some cloves; let it get cool; add to each twenty quarts of juice two quarts of cognac, and keep it in the cellar.

261. Red English Ratafia.

Four pounds of ripe, red cherries, two pounds of blackberries, three pounds of gooseberries, three pounds of raspberries, three pounds of red currants, are mashed with a wooden masher in a big earthen jug; mash in another pot one-sixteenth ounce of cloves, one-sixteenth ounce of mace, half an ounce of cinnamon, one-third ounce of coriander, one-eighth ounce of fennel, one-sixteenth ounce of Jamaica pepper, the pits of twelve apricots, the pits of twenty sour cherries, and six bitter almonds; mix the two mashes well; add two and a half quarts of sugar syrup, fill all into a large jug, close with a skin, and place it a fortnight near the stove. Then filter the juice through a linen bag, squeeze the remnants well; add one quart of best brandy to each quart of juice; place the mixture again for a fortnight near the stove; filter and bottle.

262. French Ratafia aux Quatre Fruits.

Mash ten pounds of sour cherries, eight pounds of red and two pounds of black currants, and ten pounds of raspberries; let them stand for a few days in the cellar; squeeze the juice, add the same quantity of cognac, and to each quart of the mixture one-fourth pound of refined sugar; mix all well; let the ratafia stand for a week at least; filter and bottle.

263. Another.

Mix one quart of fresh raspberry-juice, one quart of cherry-juice, one quart each of the juice of red and black currants; to each quart of juice add three quarts of cognac, seven ounces of broken lump-sugar, three cloves; expose the mixture in a large glass bottle to the sunlight until it is absolutely clear; filter and bottle.

264. Gin.

A very strong liquor manufactured in Holland (Holland gin), and England (Old Tom gin), which is distilled from juniperus berries, and is used mainly by sailors as a warming beverage, and is good for the stomach, and against scurvy. In Schiedam, Delft and Rotterdam, gin is manufactured in large quantities; in Schiedam there are more than 300 distilleries.

265. Ginger Cordial.

In a large, wide-necked bottle place one and a half ounces of pulverized ginger; infuse this in a quart of cognac, well corked, for from two to three days; stir now and then; strain through a flannel, and add a syrup of one pound of sugar cleared and refined in one gill of water; filter again; cork well.

The English often add to the pulverized ginger one pound of mashed black or white currants that secures a very delicious taste.

266. Gingerette.

One pound of very ripe black currants are cleaned from their stalks, and infused with one quart of gin, and the rind of a thinly peeled lemon three days in a well-corked bottle; strain the liquor into another bottle; add half an ounce of pulverized ginger, and one pound of granulated sugar; place the bottle in a sunny spot; shake it daily; strain the liquor once more into smaller bottles, cork well, and let them lie for a while before using.

267. Grenoble Ratafia.

Mash a quantity of very ripe sour cherries with a wooden masher, pits included; let the mash soak forty-eight hours in a clean wooden tub, then squeeze the juice. Refine the sugar, two pounds to every six or seven quarts, add the sugar syrup to the juice, one-third ounce of cloves, two-thirds of an ounce of broken cinnamon, two handfuls of fresh sour cherry leaves, and six quarts of cognac; pour everything into a small cask, which, while daily shaken, has to lie four to six weeks; bottle the ratafia after filtering; use after a while.

268. Hip Liqueur.

Infuse one and a half pounds of fresh, well-cleaned hips, cut into pieces, in one quart of kirschwasser a fortnight in a warm place; refine and clear six ounces of sugar in half a pint of boiling water; let this get cool, and mix it with the liquor; strain it through blotting-paper, and bottle it.

269. English Hop Ratafia.

A wide-necked bottle is filled with ripe, dried cones of the hop; shake them together without pressing, infuse it with sherry for four weeks; strain and mix it with a thin sugar syrup of six ounces of sugar with half a pint of water; strain again, bottle and seal; use either unmixed or with water as a tonic for the stomach.

270. Irish Usquebaugh.

(SEE WHISKEY.)

This famous cordial, which the French call Scubac, is prepared in various ways.

One and one-fifth ounces of nutmeg, as much of cloves and of cinnamon, two and one-third ounces of anise, as much of kümmel and coriander are mashed; put this with four ounces of licorice root, twenty-three quarts of rectified alcohol, and four and a half quarts of water in the distilling apparatus; color the condensated liquor with saffron, and sweeten with sugar syrup.

271. Another.

Infuse one ounce of grated nutmeg, as much of cinnamon, angelica, rhubarb and cassia; one-third ounce of saffron, as much of cardamom, cloves and mace; one-third ounce of coriander, as much of anise and kümmel, and three and one-third ounces of licorice root in twenty-three quarts of brandy a fortnight; filter the liquor; sweeten with sugar syrup, filter again and bottle; use after a few months.

272. Another.

In smaller quantities this liquor is prepared by Irish housewives as follows:

Infuse one pound of seedless raisins, half an ounce of grated nutmeg, one-fourth of an ounce of pulverized cloves, as much of cardamom, the peel of a sour orange rubbed off on sugar, half a pound of brown rock-candy, and a little saffron tincture in two quarts of brandy a fortnight; stir daily; filter and bottle.

273. Iva Liqueur.

This is very good, green bitters, which is obtained in Switzerland out of the *Achillea Moschata*, a shrub that grows on the highest Alps; it is of great aromatic odor and taste, and a great article for export.

274. Juniper Cordial.

Mash slightly half a pint of fresh juniper berries; infuse it with four quarts of cognac a fortnight in a large glass bottle; expose it to the sunlight; filter; mix with a syrup of one and a half pounds of sugar in three-fourths of a quart of water; cork well; let the mixture stand for a few days; filter and bottle.

275. Kajowsky.
(SLOE RATAFIA.)

After you have plucked, at the end of September a sufficient quantity of very ripe sloes, spread them on a sheet of paper, lay them one day in the sun, then take the pits out, wash them and dry them in the sun. For each half a pint of pits take one quart of cognac; break the pits, and put shells and pits in the cognac; let it stand for six weeks; shake now and then. Filter after this time, and fill into a large, flat tureen, then boil for each quart of liquor three pounds of loaf-sugar over a fast fire to a brownish syrup; add this carefully, while stirring, to the liquor; continue stirring until both liquids are well mixed, bottle, cork and seal.

(The longer you let it lie, the better your liquor will become.)

276. Kümmel.

Fill three quarts of cognac or kirschwasser, six ounces of broken caraway, and two-fifths of an ounce of star anise into a glass bottle, close it with a bladder, and place it in a pot partly filled with cold water; now heat this, and let boil for half an hour; take the pot from the fire, and let the bottle get cool in the water, then sweeten the liquor with two pounds of refined sugar; filter, bottle and cork well.

277. Another.

With the aid of oils the method of manufacturing is as follows:

dissolve 30 drops of caraway extract,
2 drops of fennel oil,
1 drop of cinnamon oil in one ounce of spirits; mix this to four quarts of cognac and three pounds of refined sugar; filter and bottle.

278. Lemon Ratafia.

Infuse the thinly peeled rind of four or five lemons with two quarts of cognac or kirschwasser in a corked bottle, for twelve days, in a moderately warm place; boil one and a half pounds of lump-sugar in two quarts of water until the sugar drops from the wooden spoon in large flakes; add the spirit, let it simmer over a slow fire for a few minutes, strain through flannel, and bottle after cooling.

279. English Lemon Ratafia.

Four quarts of cognac are filled into a stone jar with one and a half pounds of pulverized sugar, the juice and the rind of sixteen lemons, and two quarts of boiling milk; stir thoroughly; cover the pot and let it stand for ten days; stir the fluid daily; then strain it through flannel, and bottle.

280. Magenbitters.

Three ounces of bitter-orange peel, three-fourths of an ounce of star anise, one-fourth of an ounce of ordinary anise, half an ounce of gentian, half an ounce of alant root, one-fourth ounce of *Erythræa Centaurium*, and one-fourth ounce of cremor tartari; infuse these ingredients in four quarts of cognac two to three weeks; filter, sweeten with two pounds of refined sugar and bottle.

281. Another.

Three ounces of orange-peel, one-fourth ounce of vermouth, one-fourth ounce of *Erythræa Centaurium*, one-eighth ounce of angelica root, one-fourth ounce of violet roots, one-fourth ounce of *Carduus Benedictus*, one-eighth ounce of stick cinnamon, one-eighth ounce of grated nutmeg; infuse these ingredients in two quarts of cognac from two to three weeks; sweeten with one pound of refined sugar, and bottle.

282. Maraschino.

One of the finest liquors which is prepared in Italy and Dalmatia from the berry of the mahaleb cherry, equally excellent for its odor and taste; this fruit is black, berry-like, flat above and oval below; it tastes bitter, but contains a pit of great fragrance. When these fruits are perfectly ripe, they are gathered, and mashed together with the pits; best white honey of their own weight is added; the fluid undergoes first a fermentation, and is then subject to distillation. This first distillate has to lie for a year; then it is distilled twice more, and is now a very delicious liquor, which, however, is but the basis of the real maraschino di Zara. Take, now, sugar one-third of the liquor's weight, dissolve it in one-third of its weight of water; refine this sugar syrup by the white of one egg or more; boil it to the consistency of a thick syrup, filter through a flannel bag, and mix this with the liquor; bottle, let the bottles lie for a year, and they are filled then into the well-known straw-covered bottles that are exported from Trieste, Austria.

There is a number of recipes to imitate this cordial, but we must abstain from publishing them, as being too difficult to prepare.

283. Mint Liqueur.

Infuse two handfuls of fresh mint leaves in two quarts of the best brandy, three or four weeks, in a well-corked bottle, in the sun or in a warm place; add a cold syrup of three-fourths to one pound of sugar; filter and bottle.

284. Nalifka.

A kind of a light fruit liquor; it is made mostly of berries and cherries, but also of plums and apples, and is very highly estimated in Russia, and prepared there in almost all houses, especially in the country. The best nalifkas are won of the *Rubus Chamæmorus*, which grows only in Russia, Norway, Sweden, East Prussia, and the northern part of England, of the black and red currants, of the berries of the mountain ash, and of cherries. All these fruits must be very ripe; those of the mountain must not be gathered before the first frost.

Fill a big glass jar two-thirds full with berries, and pour over it cognac to fill the jar; close the jar with a piece of muslin; expose it from two to three months to the direct action of the sunlight, and shake every second or third day. Then filter the nalifka through a funnel covered with linen and absorbent cotton, until it flows off perfectly clear; fill into ordinary wine bottles. Add to each three or four bottles of nalifka one bottle of water, and to each bottle of the thinned liquor four ounces of sugar that has been refined in boiling water to a consistent syrup. Add to this syrup the whole quantity of nalifka, heat the fluid, while constantly stirring, nearly to the boiling-point; take it from the fire, and pour it into an earthen or china pot. After cooling, bottle, cork and seal; you may either use it right away, or keep it.

285. Nonpareil Liqueur.

Peel a perfectly ripe pineapple, cut it into slices and mash them; add twenty of the best white plums, cut in two, and without the pits—and one dozen of very aromatic pears. To each four pounds of fruit take six pounds of loaf-sugar, and one and a half quarts of water; boil all this for three-quarters of an hour in an enameled pot; pour it into a tureen, add three quarts of fine cognac, cover it air-tight, let it stand for six weeks, filter through a jelly-bag, and bottle.

286. Noyeau.

A very fine cordial; the genuine article comes from Martinique only, and is very rare and expensive; only small quantities of it must be taken, as it is not harmless at all in spite of its unique taste. It is prepared from the pits of a fruit in the West Indies, and these pits contain a strong dose of hydrocyanic acid.

The French prepare a number of very good imitations of the genuine noyeau. For those that are in possession of a distilling apparatus we add a very good French recipe:

Half a pound of cut apricot-pits are infused in six quarts of rectified alcohol, and one quart of water, for a week; distil the alcohol, mix it with one pint of orange-flower water, and three pounds of sugar that is cleared and refined in three quarts of water, filter and fill into bottles; use it after a few months.

287. English Orange Brandy.

Two pounds of lump-sugar, ten whole oranges, and one stick of cinnamon are put in five quarts of the best brandy; let it stand in a well-covered stone jar from five to six weeks, and stir it daily with a wooden spoon; filter and fill into bottles.

288. Orange-Flower Ratafia.

Three and a half ounces of fresh orange-flowers are infused in two quarts of the best brandy in a sunny place four days; filter; add a syrup of one and a half pounds of sugar in one quart of water; filter again and bottle.

289. Orange Liquor.

Peel six oranges thinly with a sharp knife, put the peel in two quarts of cognac; press the juice of the oranges on two and a half pounds of lump-sugar, which is to be added to the liquor right away after melting; let it stand five to six weeks, daily stirring with a wooden spoon; filter and fill into bottles.

290. Parfait Amour.

A very fine cordial which may be made in different ways.

If you have a distilling apparatus, distil three quarts of alcohol with the rind of four thinly peeled lemons, one-fifteenth ounce of lemon oil, one-thirtieth ounce of bergamot oil; stop when the distillate shows 60° to 70° Tralles; distil anew with one quart of milk, dye the entire distillate with cochineal tinctures lightly red, and add two quarts of sugar syrup.

BY INFUSION.

Ten drops of clove essence, five drops of nutmeg essence, and a few drops of lemon essence are mixed with two quarts of alcohol of 83°; color with cochineal tincture slightly red, and add a syrup out of four pounds of sugar in one quart of water. Let the mixture stand four weeks; stir or shake daily, then filter and bottle.

291. Another.

Mash three fine peeled celery roots with the green sprigs on them; add four and a half quarts of brandy; distil this mixture with a spoonful of salt in a retort. The obtained product is mixed with three-fourths of a pound of roasted and pulverized cocoa beans, one-fourth of an ounce of cut vanilla, and three pounds of refined sugar; let it stand for a week; color with a cochineal tincture slightly red, and filter.

292. Persico.

This fine cordial must be taken only in small doses, as it contains hydrocyanic acid. Peel half a pound of peach-pits, and half a pound of apricot-pits, mash them, and infuse the mash with one-eighth of an ounce of fine cinnamon in four quarts of cognac; infuse in a large bottle a week in the sun; filter; purify two pounds of loaf-sugar in one pint of water, strain, and let it get cool; mix this syrup with the liquor, and fill into bottles.

293. Another.

Put one and a fourth pounds of fresh peach-kernels in lukewarm water, skin and mash them; infuse the mash with one-eighth of an ounce of broken cinnamon and four quarts of best brandy in a jug for four weeks; cover the jug with a skin; after this make a syrup of two pounds of sugar and one pint of water, and filter the whole mixture through a jelly-bag; bottle.

294. Quince Liquor.

A number of very ripe, fine quinces are peeled, grated, and left over night in the cellar; the following day squeeze the juice; take to each four and a half quarts of quince-juice two quarts of cognac, one pound of sugar, one ounce of stick cinnamon, two-fifths of an ounce of cloves, and two ounces of pulverized bitter almonds; let all this stand in a well-corked bottle a fortnight; shake daily and filter.

295. Another.

Grate the quinces, let them stand twenty-four hours; squeeze the juice; refine one pound of sugar in three pints of water, add the syrup, and let all boil for a quarter of an hour; let it get cool; add the same quantity of brandy or kirschwasser, pour all into a large glass bottle, add one ounce of bitter almonds, and one and one-third ounces of coriander; let soak a fortnight; shake daily, filter and bottle.

296. English Quince Liquor.

After you have cleaned a few ripe quinces with a towel, cut them in two, cut out the seeds, and grate the fruit on a grater, place the mash lightly strewed with sugar in a large dish twenty-four hours in a cool place; squeeze the juice, filter until it is perfectly clear; add to each pint of juice half a pound of sugar, and one pint of brandy or whiskey; let the liquor stand a fortnight; shake daily and bottle.

297. French Quince Ratafia.

Very ripe, well-cleaned quinces are grated on a grater; let the mash stand three days in a well-covered earthen dish in the cellar, and squeeze the juice out. Add to the filtered juice an equal quantity of brandy, seven ounces of sugar to each quart of the mixture, a stick of cinnamon, and a few cloves; let soak two months, filter, fill into bottles and let them lie as long as possible, as the aroma is thus highly improved.

298. Raspberry Ratafia.

In a large glass bottle infuse one quart of fresh and very ripe raspberries with two quarts of cognac; close the bottle well, and let it stand in the sun four weeks; then refine two pounds of sugar in one quart of boiling water to a thin syrup; add the syrup to the liquor; strain through flannel, and bottle.

299. French Raspberry Ratafia.

Put in a tureen four quarts of cognac, two quarts of raspberry-juice, two pounds of loaf-sugar, a few sticks of cinnamon, and four or five cloves; stir it well; cover and let it stand four weeks in a warm place; strain and bottle.

300. Rose Ratafia.

One-fourth of a pound of fresh aromatic roses (leaves only) are shaken in a vessel with one pint of lukewarm water; cover well, and place aside for two days, then filter the water, and press the roses gently; mix the rose-water with the same quantity of kirschwasser; add to each quart of the mixture half a pound of refined sugar, a few coriander-kernels, and a little fine cinnamon; let the whole soak in the sun a fortnight, add some cochineal tincture for coloring, filter and bottle.

301. Rosoglio.

It is the name of several fine cordials, imported from Italy; they are prepared of orange-flowers, or other flowers and fruits, spices, etc., and exported in straw bottles from Turin, Naples, Venice, Bologna, Udine and Trieste.

An imitation of such a rosoglio is made as follows: clear and refine four pounds of sugar in one and a fourth quarts of water; mix two quarts of best alcohol of $83°$, eight drops of rose essence, two drops of cinnamon essence, two drops of lemon essence, two drops of Portugal essence, a few drops of cochineal tincture to color, with the sugar syrup; let it stand four weeks in a large bottle; filter and fill into smaller bottles.

302. Rum.

Genuine rum is a very fine liquor; it is manufactured in the West Indies out of the juice of the sugar cane, and the relics of the sugar production, as molasses and syrup: it is used all over the world for punches, grogs, teas, etc. The best rum is that of Jamaica, but the brands of St. Croix, British Guiana, Barbadoes, Antigua, and others, although they are inferior to the Jamaica rum, are very palatable. The quality of rum is best known from its aroma, its pleasing taste, and its alcohol which must amount to $58°$ to $66°$ Tralles; the best and simplest proof is, when rum is diluted in hot water or tea; then the fineness of the aroma is developed, or by rubbing a few drops between the hands.

303. Rum Liquor.

Peel the rind of two or three bitter oranges very thin; let soak for two days in one pint of cold water, filter, and refine two pounds of sugar in it; add one pint of cleared juice of the oranges, and one and a half quarts of old Jamaica rum; filter the liquor, bottle, and keep it for future use.

304. Saffron Liquor.

In a big, well-corked jug half an ounce of best saffron, one-fourth of a pound of pulverized sugar, half an ounce of broken cinnamon, half an ounce of cloves, half an ounce of Jamaica pepper, half an ounce of nutmeg (cloves, pepper, and nutmeg roughly pulverized), one ounce of sweet almonds, one-fourth of an ounce of bitter ones (both skinned and mashed with a little alcohol), one ounce of caraway, are infused in three-fourths of a quart of water and as much of the best brandy, for a fortnight; strain until perfectly clear, bottle, cork and seal; let them lie in the cellar—the longer, the better.

305. Stomach Essence.

One and a half pounds of *cortex Chinæ*, six ounces of curaçao peel, one ounce of *flores Cassiæ* are infused in four quarts of cognac from two to three weeks; filter the fluid, sweeten with two pounds of refined sugar, and bottle. (The sweetening may be omitted.)

306. Strawberry Liquor.

Fill into a large glass jar one pound of fresh strawberries, half a pound of white rock-candy (pulverized), and one and a half quarts of cognac; cork and seal well; let it stand in the sun for five weeks; shake daily, then strain the liquor through blotting-paper, and bottle.

307. Sweet Calamus Liquor.

Infuse four ounces of dried, thinly cut sweet calamus, and a little over an ounce of cut angelica in two and one-half quarts of cognac, in a well-corked, large bottle, for four weeks, in a rather warm place; clear and refine two pounds of lump-sugar in one and a half quarts of water; mix it with the liquor, filter, and bottle.

308. Vanilla Liquor.

Infuse two and a half sticks of vanilla in four quarts of brandy a fortnight; refine two pounds of sugar in four quarts of water to syrup, add the liquor; mix well over a slow fire, filter, and bottle.

309. Another.

Cut four sticks of vanilla into very small pieces, put them in a bottle with three quarts of best brandy; let infuse a fortnight, shake daily, add two pounds of refined sugar, let the liquor stand a few days, color slightly red with cochineal-tincture, and bottle.

310. Vespetro.

An Italian cordial. One-fourth of an ounce of angelica seeds, three-fourths of an ounce of coriander, one-fourth of an ounce of fennel, one-fourth of an ounce of anise, the juice and the thin peel of two lemons, and one pound of sugar are infused in two quarts of brandy five or six days, in a warm place; filter and bottle.

311. Walnut Liquor.

One pound of green walnuts gathered at the end of June or beginning of July, is cut in small pieces, and in a jug or a glass jar infused in two and a half quarts of fine brandy with one-eighth ounce of pulverized cinnamon, and as much of cloves, from six to eight weeks; cork well, and shake daily. After this time filter the infusion, add syrup of one pound of sugar and one quart of water: filter again and bottle.

312. Another.

Infuse one pound of cut green walnuts in two quarts of fine cognac, in the sun, a fortnight; filter into another bottle, add half an ounce of cinnamon, and one-fourth of an ounce of roughly pulverized cloves; let it stand another week in the sun; add a syrup of three-fourths of a pound of sugar and one pint of water; mix well, filter, and bottle; after half a year it is ready for use.

313. Whiskey Cordial.

A liquor which is made in English families, when the white currants are getting perfectly ripe.

Infuse the rind of a thinly peeled lemon, half a pint of white currants (a little mashed), and a small piece of ginger in a quart of whiskey, twenty-four hours, in a warm place; filter, sweeten with half a pound of refined sugar, filter again, and bottle.

314. Wild-Cherry Essence.

A quantity of very ripe, wild cherries are pressed through an earthen sieve with a wooden spoon, so that only the pits remain; pulverize them with a few bitter almonds; mix them with the cherry mash, and let the mixture stand two days in a cool place. After this time squeeze the juice thoroughly, let it stand for another day, strain carefully through flannel, boil it for a few seconds with lump-sugar—one pound to one quart of juice—filter again, and after cooling, bottle well and seal, and keep the bottles in a cool place.

A few spoonfuls of this extract flavor a bottle of claret or a bowl exceedingly well.

315. Whiskey.

It derives its name from the obsolete Irish word "Usquebah" or "Usquebaugh" (water of life). Another whiskey in Scotland is called "Mountain Dew." It is made from barley, but often other grains are substituted for it.

316. Peach and Apple Brandies.

They are domestic products from the juice of the corresponding fruits, and chiefly made in Maryland and New Jersey. As they are sold at high prices much adulteration is going on in them.

Punches.

Punches.

317. Admiral.

Boil one bottle of claret with one-half pound of sugar, a stick of cinnamon, and a piece of vanilla for a quarter of an hour; add the yolks of six eggs that have first been beaten in a tumbler of cold wine; beat the drink into foam over the fire, and serve it in cups.

318. Ale Flip.

This is a kind of warm beer which is very fashionable in England during the winter, and it is taken by sportsmen early in the morning before starting for the hunt. The recipe follows: one and a half quarts of ale, a spoonful of sugar, a piece of mace, half a dozen of cloves, and a small piece of butter, and let it boil; then beat the white of one egg with the yolks of two or three eggs in a spoonful of cold ale, add it to the boiling ale, and pour the whole swiftly from one vessel into another for a few minutes, then serve.

319. Ale Punch.

Take one quart of Burton ale, one glass of Niersteiner, a wineglassful of brandy, a wineglassful of capillaire syrup, the juice of a lemon, a piece of lemon-peel; grate a little nutmeg, add a piece of toast; mix everything well; let it stand cold for from two to three hours; strain, and serve.

320. Alliance de Neufchâtel.

Take the yolks of eight eggs, stir with one pound of pulverized sugar and the juice of two oranges; heat two bottles of claret with a stick of vanilla to the boiling-point; add the wine under continuous beating to the eggs and sugar, and pour the foamy drink into champagne glasses.

321. Alymeth.

Boil one bottle of Burgundy with one pound of lump-sugar, half a stick of cinnamon, a little bit of mace and coriander, and two bay-leaves; light with a burning paper, and let it burn until it goes out by itself; then fill it into glasses, and drink it warm.

322. American Punch.

Rub the peel of six lemons on one pound of sugar; squeeze the juice of the lemons and that of six oranges on it; remove the seeds carefully; add four pounds of loaf-sugar, and five cloves and two leaves of mace tied up in a piece of linen, likewise two quarts of water; refine the sugar to syrup; skim well, fill into bottles, and keep for the punch. Now mix three-fourths of a quart of green tea, one pint of cognac, one quart of old Jamaica rum, one bottle of champagne, and a cup of chartreuse well sweetened to taste with the syrup, pour it into a punch-bowl, add a big lump of ice, three oranges cut in slices, and three lemons without the seeds; let the beverage stand for two hours, stir repeatedly, and serve.

323. Ananas Punch.

Dissolve two and one-half pounds of lump-sugar in three quarts of boiling water, add three bottles of Rhine wine, one bottle of old Jamaica rum, and two bottles of champagne; let it stand on a warm stove for an hour, and add finally the juice of a mashed ananas (pineapple). Keep the vessel well covered or the aroma will escape.

324. Ananas Punch à l'Amérique.
(FOR TEN PERSONS.)

Peel and cut four pineapples of medium size, put the slices with one pound of pulverized sugar in a bowl, and let it stand well covered on a cool place, until the sugar has gone entirely into the slices; add one pint of old Jamaica rum, one pint of best brandy, one gill of curaçao, and the juice of four lemons; place a big piece of ice in the middle of the bowl; add four bottles of champagne, and serve in champagne glasses.

PUNCHES.

325. Arrack Foam.

Mix one quart of sour cream with half a pint of arrack, and four ounces of lump-sugar; beat it to foam, and serve it in glasses.

326. Arrack Punch.

Rub the peel of three or four lemons on twelve ounces of loaf-sugar, break the sugar, and dissolve it in one quart of strong, boiling tea; add the juice of six or eight lemons, and a pint of good arrack.

327. Another.

Cut six unpeeled lemons into thin slices; remove their seeds; infuse them in one pint of arrack six hours; take them out carefully with a fork without squeezing them, then dissolve one pound of lump-sugar in three pints of boiling water, add the arrack, let the beverage get cool, and serve in small glasses.

328. Beer Punch.

Boil one quart of beer with one-fourth of a pound of lump-sugar and a stick of cinnamon; beat four eggs into foam, and mix it with a wineglassful of old Jamaica rum; take the beer from the fire and add to it the mixture while continually stirring it; serve in punch glasses.

329. Beer Chaudeau.

Stir two whole eggs in a glass of wine; pour this into a pint of beer; add a teaspoonful of sugar, a stick of cinnamon, and a piece of lemon-peel; beat the whole over a fire to foam, fill it into cups, and serve.

330. Beer Grog.

Beat four eggs, pour them into one quart of beer, add one-fourth of a pound of sugar, a little cinnamon and lemon-peel; put all over a fast fire, and beat continually, until it begins to rise, without letting it boil; take it from the fire, continue beating for a few minutes, and fill into glasses.

331. English Brandy Punch.

Put the rind of two lemons in a pot with a stick of cinnamon, three-fourths of a pound of lump-sugar, some mace, and three cloves to one-half of a pint of water; let it boil slowly for ten minutes, strain it, add one bottle of brandy and the juice of the two lemons, pour into a tureen, light it, and let it burn for five minutes before filling the punch into glasses.

332. Bristol Punch.

To each quart of boiling water take the juice of one and a half lemons, the rind of half a lemon, three gills of rum, and sugar to taste. Put sugar, juice and peel in a bowl, pour over it enough water to dissolve the sugar, and to extract the aroma; after half an hour remove the peel, and add water and rum.

333. Burning Punch.

A bottle of claret, one and a half bottles of Rhine wine, one pound of sugar, and a little over one pint of rum are heated nearly to the boiling-point; take it from the fire before it boils; light with burning paper, and when the flame goes out add some hot water or tea, if you desire.

334. English Burned Punch.

Rub the rind of three lemons lightly on one pound of sugar, put the sugar in an earthen pot, and pour over it one quart of rum and one quart of claret; stir all well over a fire, until it begins to boil and the sugar is dissolved; add one quart of boiling water, and the juice of three lemons. This punch may be taken warm or cold.

335. Campichello Punch.

Heat slowly the yolks of twelve eggs with two pounds of lump-sugar on which you have rubbed off the rind of two oranges, their juice and that of three lemons, and three bottles of claret; beat it to foam until it begins to boil; then add carefully a bottle of old Jamaica rum, and serve at once.

336. Champagne Punch.

Boil one and one-half pounds of lump-sugar in three pints of water, add the juice of five lemons, half a bottle of arrack, and one bottle of champagne; heat it sufficiently, and serve

337. Champagne Crême.

Beat half a pound of pulverized sugar with the yolks of eight eggs and five whole eggs to the form of frozen snow; add, while continually beating, the rind of an orange, rubbed off on sugar, and gradually a quart-bottle of champagne; heat over a slow fire, while continually beating, and serve warm.

338. The Chat.

Boil a large pot of mixed tea; a little sugar in the bottom of a hot cup, two-thirds full of tea; fill the rest with Burgundy, and serve. If desired, add a little vanilla to the tea.

339. English Claret Punch.

Boil, in half a pint of water, half a pound of lump-sugar with one-fifth of an ounce of cinnamon, one-tenth of an ounce of pulverized ginger, and as many pulverized cloves, and the thinly peeled rind of an orange, to syrup; skim this with a wooden spoon, and add two bottles of claret; take the vessel from the fire before the wine begins to boil.

340. Cold Claret Punch.

One bottle of claret, half a pint of sherry, half a wineglassful of maraschino, the rind of a lemon, one-quarter of a pound of pulverized sugar, and a sprig of borage; let this all stand for an hour, strain the punch through a sieve, add a piece of ice and a bottle of Seltzer.

Instead of the rind of the lemon and the borage, you may add fresh raspberries and cut peaches, when these fruits are in season.

341. Claret Punch.

Pour two bottles of claret into an enameled pot, squeeze the juice of three lemons, add one pound of sugar; heat the wine to the boiling-point without letting it boil, take it from the fire, and add half a bottle of best arrack.

342. Confession of Love.

Infuse half an ounce of fine black tea in half a pint of boiling water for five minutes; decant and pour it into a tureen; rub the rind of a lemon on three pounds of lump-sugar, refine in one pint of boiling water; skim well; add a piece of vanilla, cut into small pieces, and half an ounce of dried orange-flowers; take the sugar from the fire, and leave vanilla and orange-flowers one hour in it; then strain through a sieve into a tureen. Now add a wineglassful of maraschino, the juice of five oranges, two bottles of Rhine wine, two bottles of Médoc, one bottle of Madeira, and one bottle of arrack; let the mixture get very hot, without boiling, and serve it hot; it is still better when very cold.

343. Crambambuli.

Pour one bottle of arrack into a pot, light the fluid with burning paper, and melt one pound of lump-sugar over this flame, so as to make the melting sugar drop into the fluid.

344. Cream Punch à l'Amérique.

Beat the yolks of six eggs with one pound of powdered sugar; add half a bottle of fine rum or arrack; beat one and a half quarts of milk and the whites of the six eggs to a consistent foam; mix both ingredients together, and beat again.

(This drink is very palatable, especially for ladies.)

345. Currant Shrub.

It is a kind of punch essence which, in combination with cold or hot water, furnishes a very delicious drink.

Two quarts of currants are put in a pot which is placed in a larger one partly filled with water; let it slowly boil until the berries burst and the juice flows out; skim well and filter; to each pint of juice take three-fourths pound of sugar; dissolve it well, and add one quart of old Jamaica rum; filter the mixture again, bottle, and seal.

346. Egg Grog.

Boil one quart of water with half a pound of sugar; beat the yolks of five eggs in one pint of St. Croix rum, and add this, while continually stirring, to the boiling water.

347. Egg Punch.

Six eggs, and the yolks of ten eggs are well stirred in a new enameled pot, with one and one-fourth pounds of powdered sugar; add, while continually stirring, one bottle of Rhine wine and one quart of cold water; put over a coal-fire, and beat until it boils; add the juice of two oranges and of two lemons, and half a bottle of arrack; beat again until boiling, strain through a sieve, and serve.

348. Egg Liquor.

Put in a tureen the yolks of twelve fresh eggs, one pound of pulverized sugar, a small teaspoonful of powdered cinnamon, and a little grated nutmeg; place the tureen on ice; beat the yolks to foam, and add, while beating, one pint of kirschwasser and three pints of sweet cream; beat the mixture for another quarter of an hour, strain through a sieve, and serve in glasses.

349. Egg Milk Punch.

Infuse a stick of vanilla in one quart of boiling milk; strain the milk, add six ounces of sugar and one quart of sweet cream: let this boil up once more; stir into it the yolks of five or six eggs; let the fluid get cool, and add one pint of Santa Cruz rum.

350. Egg-Nogg Punch.

Beat well the yolks of four eggs in a tureen with six ounces of powdered sugar; add gradually one pint of fine brandy, one-fifth of a pint of Santa Cruz rum, one pony of maraschino, and two quarts of milk; beat the whites of the eggs till they assume a light, snowy appearance, and sweeten with a little vanilla or lemon sugar; let the whites float on top of the mixture; put it on ice, and serve cold.

351. Egg Punch.

Take one bottle of Rhine wine, the juice of two lemons and their peel rubbed on six ounces of lump-sugar, ten eggs, and nine ounces of pulverized sugar; stir all well; place the pot in a vessel partly filled with boiling water, beat the mixture to a thick foam, and add finally half a pint of warmed arrack.

352. Cold Egg Punch.

Pour three-fourths of a quart of boiling water on one ounce of fine black tea; let it stand for about six minutes; strain the tea, sweeten with four ounces of sugar, add the well-beaten yolks of five eggs, and stir thoroughly; fill it into a freezing-can, and turn it in the ice-cream freezer for ten minutes; add the juice of two lemons and two oranges, and turn again for a quarter of an hour; three-quarters of an hour before serving the punch begin anew to turn and stir the whole mixture, so as to make it flowing and foamy. Finally beat the whites of the five eggs to foam; mix it with one-fourth pound of sugar, add it to the punch, and half a pint of Santa Cruz rum, and serve in glasses.

353. Cold Egg Wine.

The yolks of seven fresh eggs are stirred with two ounces of powdered sugar and a teaspoonful of lemon-juice; add this to two quarts of cold Rhine wine while briskly and continually stirring.

354. Egg Wine.

One pint of white wine, the yolks of two fresh eggs, two ounces of pulverized sugar, are well mixed, and beaten over fire until the wine rises.

355. Another.

Boil one pint of Rhine wine, half a pint of water, and two ounces of sugar; meanwhile stir the yolks of two eggs in two tablespoonfuls of cold water; add the boiling wine while continually beating or stirring, and serve in glasses.

356. English Punch.

Rub the rind of two large lemons on half a pound of sugar; put it in a tureen, squeeze the juice of the fruit on it, pour one quart of boiling water over it; stir all well; add three gills of rum, half a pint of best brandy; grate a little nutmeg, heat it over a coal fire, but do not let it boil, and fill into glasses.

357. Another.

Rub the rind of two lemons, and of one bitter orange on seven ounces of sugar; put it in a tureen, squeeze the juice of the fruit over it, add one and a half pints of boiling water, stir until the sugar is dissolved, add one pint of rum, half a pint of brandy, and two tablespoonfuls of noyeau, and serve in glasses.

358. Another.

One ounce of tea is steeped in two quarts of boiling water; strain the tea over three-fourths pound of lump-sugar, on which the rind of four or five bitter oranges has been rubbed off; add a bottle of Santa Cruz rum, and serve.

359. Fletsch.

Rub the rind of three lemons on twelve ounces of lump-sugar, add two quarts of boiling water, and three quarts of hot claret, and serve as soon as the sugar is dissolved.

360. Flip.

One and a half quarts of beer are heated to boiling, with a stick of cinnamon, a small piece of ginger, two or three cloves, and some lemon-peel; meanwhile mix the yolks of four eggs with a large wineglassful of rum or arrack, two or three tablespoonfuls of pulverized sugar, and a small spoonful of corn-starch; add this, while continually stirring, to the beer; pour it a few times from one vessel into another, strain through a sieve, and serve in cups.

361. Fruit Punch.

Boil three quarts of water with twelve ounces of sugar, and the juice of two or three lemons; mix this in a tureen with one quart of Santa Cruz rum or arrack, and one quart of raspberry or cherry syrup.

362. George IV. Punch.

On seven ounces of sugar rub the peel of two lemons, and of two bitter oranges; put in a tureen with the juice of the fruits; let it stand for half an hour; add one cup of boiling water, and stir until the sugar is dissolved. Add one pint of green tea, half a pint of pineapple syrup, a wineglassful of maraschino, four tablespoonfuls of the best arrack, one pint of brandy, and a bottle of champagne; mix all, put on ice, and serve.

363. German Tea Punch.

Heat one quart of white beer with a little stick of cinnamon, add a spoonful of corn-starch dissolved in wine; stir rapidly; add half a bottle of Rhine wine, six ounces of sugar, and the juice of half a lemon; heat all once more to the boiling-point; beat the yolks of four eggs with it; sweeten with one pound of sugar on which you have previously rubbed off the rind of half a lemon; add a pony of maraschino, and serve in cups.

364. Another.

Heat two quarts of white beer, beat in it the yolks of six eggs; add three-fourths pound of sugar, on which you have rubbed the rind of half a lemon, and half a bottle of white wine; heat the mixture again, while continually beating, but do not let it boil; add half a wineglassful of maraschino, and the juice of a lemon; serve very foamy in cups.

365. Gin Punch.

Peel the rind of a large lemon very thin, put it with a tablespoonful of the juice of a lemon in a tureen, add two tablespoonfuls of powdered sugar, and one pint of cold water, and let it stand for half an hour; afterward add half a pint of the best Holland gin, a wineglassful of maraschino, three or four lumps of ice, two bottles of plain soda, and serve at once.

366. Giroflée.

Boil two bottles of Médoc with one pound of lump-sugar, one stick of cinnamon, and some cloves for a few minutes

367. Glasgow Punch.

Put half a pound of pulverized sugar, and the rind of half a thinly peeled lemon with the juice of two large lemons in a tureen, add a bottle of old Jamaica rum, and five quarts of boiling water; stir well, and servè in glasses.

368. Grog.

Take a quart of boiling tea with half a pound of lump-sugar, and add one pint of Santa Cruz rum or arrack.

369. Holland Punch.

Strain the juice of three or four fine lemons; mix it with one pound of powdered sugar, and one bottle of fine Holland gin; let it stand well covered in a warm place until the sugar is dissolved; add two and a half quarts of boiling water, stir all thoroughly and serve.

370. Hong Kong Punch.

A pound of loaf-sugar in a large enameled pot, the juice of six peeled lemons, the juice of three peeled oranges, one quart of cold water, one bottle of Jamaica rum, half a pint of brandy, one quart bottle of Burgundy; put this over a slow fire, and stir until boiling, then boil about one gallon of mixed tea; mix this all together—hot—and serve. If desired, beat up the whites of three eggs to the form of snow, and use a little of this for the top of each portion. If not sweet enough add sugar to taste.

371. Cold Hoppelpoppel.

The yolks of four eggs and a little ground nutmeg are stirred into half a pint of cold, sweet cream, and beaten to a thick foam; add one gill of Santa Cruz rum, and sweeten to taste.

372. Hot Hoppelpoppel.

One quart of sweet cream and two tablespoonfuls of powdered sugar are heated to the boiling-point; into a little milk stir the yolks of four fresh eggs, and beat all to a thick foam; finally add half a pint of rum. Serve in glasses or cups.

Instead of cream you may use boiling water or tea.

373. Hot Wine.

Heat one quart of good claret with six ounces of lump-sugar, a stick of cinnamon, six cloves, and the rind of a thinly peeled lemon; let it boil for a moment; strain and serve in glasses.

374. Another.

Boil the rind of a lemon, one-fourth ounce of stick cinnamon, and eight cloves in one pint of water very slowly for half an hour; add two bottles of claret; sweeten all with one pound of lump-sugar; place the well-covered pot in boiling water until the wine boils; strain and serve.

375. Hot Wine à la Française.

Boil three bottles of Bordeaux or Roussillon in an enameled pot with one pound of sugar, one-third ounce of stick cinnamon, two or three leaves of mace, and six bay-leaves; take it from the fire, and light it with a burning paper; let it burn for three minutes, strain, and serve in glasses.

376. Hunters' Punch.

Two bottles of Moselle or light Rhine wine and half a bottle of arrack punch essence are slowly heated in a well-covered enameled pot; heat sufficiently, but avoid boiling; a white, delicious foam will be formed on top, then serve in cut glasses.

377. Iced Punch.

Refine and clear one pound of lump-sugar in one pint of water; let the syrup get cool; add the juice of four or five lemons, and the rind of two rubbed off on sugar; let the mixture freeze in the ice-cream freezer, and add then, while continually turning, a bottle of Rhine wine or champagne, half a pint of Santa Cruz rum or arrack, and half a pony of maraschino; serve the thickly flowing punch in glasses.

378. Imperial Punch.

Peel one pineapple and four oranges; cut the first into small slices, and separate the oranges into pieces; put all in a tureen; then boil in a quart of water two sticks of cinnamon and a stick of vanilla, cut into small pieces; strain the water through a sieve into the tureen; rub the rind of a lemon on one and a half pounds of lump-sugar, put the sugar into the water, and squeeze the juice of three lemons; cover well; let it get cool, place it on ice, add a bottle of Rhine wine, one quart of fine rum, and, shortly before serving, a bottle of champagne and half a bottle of Seltzer.

379. Ladies' Punch.

Put in a tureen the thinly peeled rind and the juice of three blood-oranges, the juice of four lemons with one quart of water; cover, and let it stand for three hours; strain the fluid; add one quart of purified sugar syrup, one quart of brandy, one pint of Santa Cruz rum, and the decoction of half an ounce of stick cinnamon in one and a half quarts of boiling water; heat the punch by placing the tureen in a larger vessel partly filled with water, and serve in glasses.

380. Lemon Punch.

Refine and clear one pound of lump-sugar in one pint of water, and boil it with the rind of a thinly peeled lemon and the juice of three lemons to the consistency of syrup; let it get cool; add three bottles of Rhine wine, three gills of arrack, one pint of light tea; strain through flannel; heat it without boiling, and serve.

381. Another.

Rub the rind of two lemons on half a pound of sugar, add a decoction of one and a half quarts of water and half an ounce of fine tea; squeeze the juice of four lemons; strain; add one pint of old Jamaica rum; heat it once more, and serve.

382. Malinverno Punch.

Clear and refine one pound of sugar in one quart of water; boil one pound of barberries—ripe and well-cleaned—after you have mashed them with a wooden spoon, in the refined sugar syrup; add a bottle of claret, press all through a sieve; add a bottle of Santa Cruz rum, and some raspberry syrup, and you may serve the punch hot or cold.

383. Manhattan Punch.

(HOT OR COLD.)

Take a large enameled pot, the juice of six lemons, the juice of two oranges, a pound of sugar, two quarts of cold water, two quarts of claret, two or three sticks of cinnamon, two dozen cloves, half a pint of Jamaica rum or brandy; place this over a slow fire until boiling; strain carefully before serving. You may serve it hot; if not, you may bottle it, and it will keep for several days.

384. Maraschino Punch.

Three to four bottles of Rhine wine and half a bottle of arrack are mixed with half a bottle of maraschino di Zara and two pounds of cleaned and refined sugar—cold; place the punch for a couple of hours on ice, and add a bottle of champagne just before serving.

385. Maurocordato.

Heat one and a half quarts of sweet cream with a piece of vanilla and half a pound of sugar to the boiling-point; let it then steep for a while; strain the cream through a sieve; beat it with the yolks of six or eight eggs; add enough fine arrack or maraschino to taste.

386. Mecklenburg Punch.

Rub the peel of two lemons on two pounds of sugar; add one and a half quarts of good tea, four bottles of claret, one bottle of French white wine, and one bottle of brandy; let everything get hot over a slow fire; stir well, and serve.

387. Another.

Two pounds of sugar on which two lemons are rubbed off, four bottles of Bordeaux, one bottle of port wine, one bottle of brandy, and half a bottle of Madeira.

388. English Milk Punch.

Rub the peel of three fine lemons on one pound of lump-sugar; put it in a tureen, and squeeze the juice of the fruit over it; grate half a nutmeg; add a bottle of Jamaica rum; mix all thoroughly, and let it stand well covered over night. Then add one quart of boiling water, and one quart of boiling milk; let the mixture stand covered two hours; filter through a canton flannel bag, in which you placed a piece of blotting-paper, until the punch is absolutely clear, and drink it cold.

389. Another.

Rub the peel of two lemons on one and a half pounds of lump-sugar; put this in a tureen; add gradually the juice of the two lemons, a quart of hot milk, one quart of hot water, some pieces of vanilla, cut into small pieces, a little grated nutmeg, and a bottle of good arrack, and let the well-covered tureen stand over night. The following morning you filter the thick fluid through a flannel bag, until it gets clear; fill into bottles, and serve the punch cold; it may be kept as long as you please.

390. Another.

In a bottle of fine rum put the thinly peeled rind of three oranges and three lemons; cork the bottle well, and let the bottle stand two days. After this rub the rind of six lemons on two pounds of loaf-sugar, squeeze their juice and that of the formerly peeled lemons and oranges over the sugar; add two quarts of boiling water, one and a half quarts of boiling milk, and half a teaspoonful of grated nutmeg, and mix all well until the sugar is dissolved. Now add the rum; strain the punch until it is perfectly clear; fill into bottles, and cork them very well.

Such a milk-punch is a beverage refreshing and harmless, which, in summer especially, for excursions, picnics, etc., cannot be too highly appreciated.

391. Finland Milk Punch.

This punch is prepared like our first "English Milk Punch;" only take Santa Cruz rum instead of Jamaica rum, and leave the nutmeg out.

392. Warm Milk Punch.

A quart of fresh milk is slowly heated to boiling with the thin peel of a small lemon; then strain the milk, beat it with the yolks of four eggs, stirred up beforehand in cold milk; add a wineglassful of brandy, and two wineglassfuls of rum; beat all over a slow fire to foam, and fill into glasses.

393. Nectar Punch à l'Amérique.
(FOR BOTTLING.)

Infuse the rind of fifteen thinly peeled lemons forty-eight hours in one and a half pints of rum; filter; add two quarts of cold water and three pints of rum, the juice of the lemons, a grated nutmeg, and two and a half quarts of boiling milk; cover well, let stand for twenty-four hours, and sweeten with three pounds of sugar; strain through a flannel bag, until the punch is perfectly clear, and bottle.

394. Negus.

This beverage is of English origin, and there very highly estimated; it derives its name from its inventor, the English Colonel Negus.

Put the rind of half a lemon or orange in a tureen, add eight ounces of sugar, one pint of port wine, the fourth part of a small nutmeg—grated; infuse this for an hour; strain; add one quart of boiling water, and the drink is ready for use.

395. Another.

In other countries they are used to take lighter wines. The recipe follows: Put two bottles of claret, two sticks of cinnamon, six cloves, a little pulverized cardamom, a little grated nutmeg, and half a pound of sugar, on which you have previously rubbed the rind of a lemon, on a slow fire; cover well, and heat to the boiling-point; strain through a hair-sieve; add one pint of boiling water, and the juice of one and a half lemons, and serve in strong glasses, that are first warmed.

396. Norfolk Punch.

Infuse the rind of fifteen lemons and of as many oranges, thinly peeled, in two quarts of brandy or rum for forty-eight hours; filter the infusion, and add it to the cold syrup of two pounds of sugar and two and a half quarts of water; squeeze the juice of the lemons and oranges; pour all into a great stone jug, tie with a bladder, and let it stand for from six to eight weeks before using.

397. Nuremberg Punch.

Rub lightly the peel of an orange on three-fourths pound of sugar; squeeze the juice of two oranges on it; pour one quart of boiling water over it; add a small pint of good old arrack, and a bottle of old Bordeaux—hot, but not boiling; mix all well, and serve.

398. Orange Punch.

Rub the peel of three oranges on sugar; place the sugar in a pot; add the juice of six oranges and two lemons, one pound of lump-sugar, one bottle of white wine, one quart of water; let all boil; pour it into a bowl, and add two bottles of white wine, and one and a half pints of arrack or rum.

399. Prince of Wales Punch.
(COLD.)

In a small bowl put the thinly peeled and cut rind of half a lemon, and two and a half ounces of granulated sugar; add one-fourth quart of boiling water; let it stand for a quarter of an hour; add a bottle of champagne, and a gill of the best arrack; mix the fluids well, and place the bowl on ice one or two hours.

400. Port Wine Punch.

A bottle of claret, a bottle of Rhine wine, and a bottle of port wine are heated with two pounds of sugar, until the sugar is dissolved; do not let it boil; meanwhile squeeze the juice of four lemons into a tureen, add half a bottle of fine arrack and the sweet mixture; stir well, and serve.

401. Punch à la Diable.

Place on the stove a large enameled pot, in which, before, water had been boiling; lay on it two flat iron bars, and place on these two pounds of lump-sugar; pour over the sugar a bottle of old Jamaica rum, and light it carefully with a burning paper, to let the melting sugar flow into the pot; when the flame goes out by itself, add three bottles of Rhine wine, and one quart of black tea, the juice of one lemon and of one orange; let it stand covered three hours in a warm, but not hot oven.

402. Punch à l'Empereur.

Rub on three pounds of lump-sugar the rind of one orange and one lemon; squeeze the juice of four lemons on the sugar; boil in one and a half quarts of water, until it becomes clear; add half a bottle of arrack, one bottle of Rhine wine, and one bottle of Burgundy, and let the punch simmer for a while without letting it boil; then serve.

403. Punch à la Crême.

Dissolve four pounds of sugar in four quarts of hot water; heat this with four quarts of arrack, the juice of eight lemons, and a small piece of vanilla, cut in pieces, in an enameled pot to the boiling-point; as soon as this is reached add three quarts of milk or cream, while constantly stirring. Take the vessel from the fire, tie a cloth over it, let it stand for two hours; filter, bottle, and keep it for future use, as it may be preserved for a very long time.

404. Punch à la Bavaroise.

Rub the rind of three lemons on one pound of lump-sugar; squeeze the juice of the fruit on it; add one quart of water and two bottles of Burgundy; heat slowly to the boiling-point; filter through canton flannel, and serve it hot.

405. Punch à la Ford.

Three dozen lemons are very thinly peeled; the rind is put in an enameled pot, three pounds of sugar added, and all is stirred for about half an hour; add five quarts of boiling water; stir until the sugar is dissolved; add to each three quarts one pint of the best Jamaica rum and one pint of brandy; bottle the punch, keep it in the cellar, and use it after the expiration of some weeks—the later the better.

406. Punch à la Française.

Put one and a half pounds of lump-sugar in a new earthen pot, pour over it one quart of rum; light this, and let burn until the sugar becomes brown and is melted to one-third of its original volume; add three-fourths quart of boiling tea, the juice of six lemons and of six oranges; stir well, and serve at once.

407. Another.

Two pounds of sugar in an earthen pot are mixed with half a glass of water or tea, the juice of two lemons and two oranges, and cleared and refined to syrup; add a bottle of rum, a bottle of brandy, and tea, until the punch receives the required mildness. Heat, and, before serving, squeeze the juice of six oranges through a sieve.

408. Punch à la Régence.

The thinly peeled rind of two lemons and two bitter oranges are put in a tureen with some vanilla, and as much cinnamon, and four cloves, poured over with the boiling syrup of one and a half pounds of sugar and three-fourths quart of water, and placed aside for two hours. Add the purified juice of twelve lemons, one bottle of old Jamaica rum, and half a bottle of brandy; filter the punch through a cloth, fill into bottles, and place the bottles on ice.

409. Punch à la Reine.

Rub the rind of two or three lemons off on one-fourth pound of sugar, squeeze the juice of six lemons and two oranges on it; add a syrup of three-fourths pound of sugar and three gills of water; after all is well mixed let it freeze in the freezing-can; mix a cup of rum and as much brandy to the ice, likewise the thick foam of the whites of three eggs, sweetened with vanilla-sugar; leave the punch for a while in the freezing-can, and serve.

410. Punch à la Romaine.

Rub the rind of two oranges and one lemon on one and a half pounds of sugar; put it in a tureen, and add one pint of water; when the sugar is properly dissolved add the juice of four oranges and two lemons, half a bottle of Rhine wine, half a pint of arrack, half a pint of maraschino, and a pint-bottle of champagne; place the mixture in the freezing-can, turn continually, and let it freeze; finally, stir the froth of the whites of five eggs, sweetened with sugar, to it; let all freeze for a while, until it looks like thick cream; serve in champagne glasses.

411. Another.

Rub the peel of six lemons off on sugar; squeeze the juice of the lemons and of two oranges; add half a pint of water and one pint of sugar-syrup out of three-fourths pound of sugar and one pint of water; stir all well, and let it freeze in the freezing-can. Then mix the solid froth of the whites of four eggs with half a pound of pulverized sugar; add this, with three gills of brandy, a bottle of champagne, and a cup of green tea, to the ice; mix all thoroughly; leave the punch for a short while in the freezing-can, and serve in glasses.

412. Punch à la Tyrolienne.

The thin peel of four lemons, half an ounce of stick cinnamon, six cloves, two pounds of sugar, one and a half quarts of water are heated over a slow fire until the sugar is dissolved. Add the juice of eight lemons, two quarts of claret, one bottle of arrack, one quart of white wine; heat it once more to the boiling-point, and serve.

413. Raspberry Punch.

Two quarts of moderately strong black tea are mixed with one pint of raspberry-juice, and heated; then dissolve in it two pounds of sugar; let the fluid boil for a few seconds; add one quart of arrack de Batavia, and serve at once.

414. Another.

Add to half a pint of raspberry syrup three and one-half pints of boiling water, half a pint of Santa Cruz rum, and half a pint of brandy; sweeten to taste; add a pony of maraschino; stir well, and serve.

415. Rhine Wine Punch.

Heat three bottles of Rhine wine nearly to boiling; add one quart of strong tea, twelve ounces of sugar on which you have rubbed the rind of a lemon, the juice of the lemon, and one or two gills of fine arrack; mix all well, and serve.

416. Another.

Heat very slowly six bottles of Rhine wine, three-fourths quart of old Jamaica rum, one and three-fourths to two pounds of sugar nearly to the boiling-point, and serve hot.

417. Royal Punch.

Three pounds of lump-sugar are put in a tureen, then pour over it one quart of light hot tea—as soon as the sugar is perfectly dissolved squeeze in the juice of three lemons and three oranges; add one pint of fine Rhine wine, as much Bordeaux, champagne, arrack, maraschino, and pineapple syrup; mix all very well, and place the tureen, well covered, on ice.

418. Rum Punch.

Put two pounds of sugar in a tureen; squeeze on it the juice of five lemons, add the thin peel of two lemons, and three quarts of boiling water. After the sugar is dissolved add a bottle of old Jamaica rum, and a bottle of champagne, and serve cold or hot.

419. Russian Punch.

Rub the peel of four lemons and of four oranges off on two pounds of sugar; put it in a tureen; add the juice of the fruits, and one and a half quarts of cold water; let the tureen stand until the sugar is melted; fill all in a freezing-can, and prepare ice-cream of it. Then add gradually one bottle of champagne, and half a bottle of arrack; mix all well, and serve in glasses.

420. Sapazeau.

Rub the yellow rind of four fine oranges lightly on half a pound of loaf-sugar; pulverize; put in a kettle; squeeze the juice of the fruit on it; add six eggs, and the yolks of four; beat them well; add one and a half quarts of Rhine wine, and beat all over a slow fire to a thick, boiling mass. Take the Sapazeau from the fire, mix with a small cup of maraschino, and serve hot in cups or glass mugs.

421. Snow-Flakes.

Two bottles of Moselle or Rhine wine are slowly heated with some lemon-peel and four ounces of sugar. Beat the whites of four eggs with a little powdered sugar and some lemon extract to a thick foam; with a spoon take off small snowballs from the foam, and place them in the boiling wine; take them out again carefully with a lifter; then stir the yolks of the eggs in a little wine, and add it to the hot wine while continually stirring. Pour the wine in a bowl; place the snowballs on top, and grate a little cinnamon.

422. Sporting Punch.

A bottle of brandy, half a pint of Jamaica rum, half a pint of peach brandy, a wineglassful of curaçao, one-fourth pound of sugar—dissolved in hot water; mix all this in a bowl; add a lump of ice, and serve.

423. Steel Punch.

Infuse a small stick of vanilla, some stick cinnamon, and two cloves in half a pint of water on a warm place, about 200° F., well covered; filter into an enameled pot; add one quart of claret, five ounces of powdered sugar, and stir very well; make an iron red hot, hold it in the fluid until it gets cold; stir the yolks of six eggs in a little claret, add them, and beat all to foam over a slow fire.

424. Strawberry Punch.

Two quarts of fine, ripe strawberries are mashed in a stone pot; add one bottle of Santa Cruz rum; tie it closely, and let it stand three days; stir once a day; strain and squeeze through canton flannel; now put one pound of granulated sugar in a bowl; press the juice of two lemons thereon; pour the rum over it, and add finally three quarts of boiling water; cover the bowl well, and do not serve before the punch is perfectly cold.

425. "Texas Siftings" Punch.

Pare off the peel of four blood-oranges very thin; pour over it a large glass of white wine; let soak for half a day in a well-covered tureen; strain the wine into a bowl; add two bottles of good Bordeaux, two bottles of Rhine or Moselle wine, and two bottles of champagne; sweeten to taste; mix all well, and serve in glasses.

426. Uhles.

A bottle of white wine, as much water, and four ounces of sugar are heated to the boiling-point; the yolks of six eggs beaten into it to a thick foam, mixed with two wineglassfuls of arrack; serve in glass mugs.

427. United Service Punch.

In one and a fourth quarts of hot, strong tea dissolve one pound of sugar; add the juice of six lemons, one pint of arrack, and one pint of port wine; warm up, and serve.

428. Vin Brulé.

Two bottles of white wine with three-fourths pound of sugar, on which the peel of two lemons was rubbed off, the juice of the lemons, and a piece of cinnamon are placed over a slow fire in a well-covered new earthen pot; just before boiling add, through a hair-sieve, the yolks of eight or ten eggs, beaten in a little wine; take it from the fire, and serve in glasses.

429. Washington's Punch.

The juice of six lemons in a large bowl, a pound of sugar, a pint of Jamaica rum, a pint of brandy, one and a half pints of black tea; add five or six bottles of champagne; mix this well; add some sliced oranges and pineapples, one large piece of ice, and serve.

430. Whiskey Punch.

Rub the rind of three lemons on seven ounces of sugar; put the sugar in a tureen; add one quart of boiling water and the juice of the fruit; this syrup is mixed with one pint or more of old Irish whiskey.

431. Whist.

Half an ounce of Pecco tea is infused in one pint of boiling water; pour the tea through a hair-sieve upon one pound of sugar; squeeze the juice of five or six lemons, and mix all with three quarts of very good Bordeaux; heat without boiling, and serve in glasses.

Bowls.

Bowls.

432. Ananas Bowl.

Peel a fresh pineapple, cut it into slices; place that in a large bowl, and cover with one pound of pulverized sugar; cover the bowl well, and let it stand from twelve to twenty-four hours; add, according to the number of guests, three, four, or more bottles of Rhine wine; for every bottle of wine add six ounces of lump-sugar; place on ice, and add, before serving, a bottle of champagne.

433. Ananas Cardinal.

Peel a fresh pineapple; cut it into slices; put that in a bowl, sugar it well, pour in one bottle of Rhine wine, and let it stand for a couple of hours; add, then, according to the number of guests, three or four bottles of Rhine wine; put it on ice, and serve.

434. Ananas Julep.

Peel a ripe pineapple; cut it into thin slices, and place that in a bowl; add the juice of two oranges, one gill of raspberry syrup, one gill of maraschino, one gill of old Holland gin, one bottle of sparkling Moselle wine, and a scoop of shaved ice; mix thoroughly, and fill into glasses.

435. Apple Bowl.

Peel twelve good, juicy, aromatic apples; remove the seeds; cut them into thin slices; put in a tureen thickly strewed with fine sugar; cover the tureen well, and let it stand in a cool place twenty-four hours; add a wineglassful of old Jamaica rum, and let it stand again for two hours; pour three to four bottles of a light Moselle or Rhine wine over it; put the tureen on ice for a few hours; strain the wine through flannel, and add one bottle of champagne.

436. Badminton.

Peel one-half of a cucumber of medium size; cut into rather thick slices; put them in a bowl; add six ounces of pulverized sugar; grate a little nutmeg on top of it, and add a bottle of claret; put the bowl on ice, and add, after stirring, a siphon of Seltzer.

437. English Beer Bowl.

Infuse the peel of a lemon, a thin slice of toast, some ground nutmeg and some pulverized ginger in a large wineglassful of brandy; add a sprig of borage, one of pimpernel, and some slices of peeled apples; pour over it two quarts of porter or ale, sweeten with three tablespoonfuls of sugar; cool it, and serve with cheese, bread and butter.

438. Cold Bishop.

Peel a green, bitter orange very thin; put that in a new earthen pot; infuse it in one bottle of best Bordeaux or Burgundy in the well-covered pot from ten to twelve hours; strain, and sweeten at discretion.

439. English Bishop.
(WARM.)

Make slight incisions into the rind of four small, bitter oranges; roast them before a fire, on a grate, on both sides; place them in an enameled pot; add two bottles of fine claret, a few pieces of cinnamon and a fried bread-crust; cover the pot well, and let it simmer from six to eight hours; strain the wine through flannel, and sweeten to taste and serve.

440. Russian Bishop.

Peel the rind of four bitter oranges; put in a tureen and infuse with three bottles of Muscat Lunel for an hour; strain the wine through flannel; bottle, and place on ice for one or two hours; then serve in glasses.

441. Cardinal.

Peel four bitter oranges with a sharp knife, very carefully; infuse the peel with four bottles of Rhine wine for ten hours; sweeten with one and a half pounds of sugar; put it on ice; strain and serve.

442. Another.

Take two bitter and two sweet oranges; rub the rind of them on one and a half pounds of lump-sugar; put the sugar in a bowl; press the juice of the two sweet oranges over it; add a bottle of white wine; put it on ice; strain and serve.

443. Another.

Peel three small oranges; put the rind in a bowl and pour a bottle of Moselle wine over it; strain the wine after eight hours; press the juice of seven or eight oranges on two pounds of lump-sugar; let the sugar melt in the first bottle of Moselle wine; add three others and a bottle of port wine; a little ananas syrup will increase exceedingly the taste of the bowl.

444. Celery Bowl à l'Amérique.

Peel three or four fresh celery-roots; cut them into thin slices; cover them in a bowl thickly with powdered sugar; infuse with half a bottle of brandy, arrack, or rum, well covered, for twelve hours; strain, and add four bottles of Rhine wine and one bottle of champagne; put it for two hours on ice, and add, before serving, a scoop of fine ice.

445. English Cider Bowl.

Make an extract of a spoonful of green tea in a half-pint of boiling water; let it stand for fifteen minutes; pour it into a bowl; add six ounces of lump-sugar, one bottle of cider, two wineglassfuls of brandy, half a pint of cold water, a couple of fresh cucumber slices, some leaves of borage, and two leaves of Roman sage, and place the bowl on ice.

446. Another.

Peel a lemon or orange very thin; infuse the rind in a cup of boiling water in a bowl; add some borage-leaves, some cucumber slices, some sprigs of balm, half a pound of sugar, one pint of sherry, Madeira or Malaga (or, instead of this, two wineglassfuls of brandy), and two bottles of cider; put the bowl on ice and serve.

447. Champagne Bowl.

To one pound of lump-sugar add two bottles of Moselle wine, one bottle of Burgundy and two bottles of champagne; cover the bowl well and put it on ice.

448. Sherry Bowl.

The rind of six lemons is infused four hours in one-fourth quart of boiling water; pour this water in a bowl; add the juice of two lemons, one pint of sherry, three gills of old Jamaica rum, three gills of brandy, one pound of lump-sugar, three pints of cold water, and one pint of boiling milk; mix everything thoroughly; strain it through flannel, and put it for four hours on ice.

449. English Claret Bowl.

Peel an orange and cut it in slices, likewise half a cucumber; add a few sprigs of borage and balm, two or three tablespoonfuls of pulverized sugar, a wineglassful of brandy, or two glasses of sherry, two bottles of claret, and a bottle of Seltzer; stir everything well, put it two hours on ice, and strain before serving.

450. English Gin Bowl.

Put the rind of a thinly peeled lemon and its juice in a tureen, add three tablespoonfuls of powdered sugar, and one quart of water, and let it stand an hour; pour over it one pint of Old Tom gin, a wineglassful of maraschino, three tablespoonfuls of shaved ice, and a bottle of Seltzer, and serve.

451. Hippocras.

A kind of spiced wine of the mediæval age, when one did not yet understand blending the wines, consequently they always were of a certain acidity, which was covered by addition of honey and spices. A recipe for manufacturing hippocras, which Talleyraut, the head cook of Charles VII., king of France, has made, reads as follows: To a quart of wine take one-third of an ounce of very fine and clean cinnamon, one-thirtieth ounce of ginger, twice as much of cloves, as much of nutmeg, and six ounces of sugar and honey; grind the spices, put them in a muslin bag, hang this in the wine for ten to twelve hours, and filter several times.

Wherever, nowadays, hippocras is made, it is made in the following manner: Cut eight to ten large, aromatic, well-peeled apples into thin slices; put that in a tureen, add half a pound of sugar, three or four pepper kernels, the rind of a lemon, one-third of an ounce of whole cinnamon, two ounces of peeled and mashed almonds, and four cloves; pour over this two bottles of Rhine wine, cover it well, and let it soak with the other ingredients; filter the wine, and you may use this wine also for a bowl.

452. Linden Blossom Bowl.

Pluck fully developed linden blossoms; look carefully that no insects are on them; put them in a tureen; pour over that two bottles of Rhine wine; cover the tureen well, and let it stand from six to eight hours; strain, and add wine according to the number of guests; sweeten to taste, and add finally a pint bottle of champagne or a bottle of Seltzer.

453. May Bowl.

For the preparation of this favorite spring beverage there is a number of more or less complicated recipes, of which we first give the simplest one, and afterwards some of the more complicated ones.

Put a handful of woodruff (*asperula odorata*) that has no blossoms yet, in a bowl; pour over it two bottles of Moselle wine, cover the bowl, let it soak not longer than half an hour in a very cool place; take the woodruff out, sweeten with from four to five ounces of sugar, stir well, and serve the aromatic beverage at once. You improve the fine taste by adding the thin slices of one or two peeled oranges. If you prepare this delicious beverage in this simple way, it is the best, as the unadulterated aroma of the woodruff is obtained; but take care that you do not leave the herb too long in the wine or you will get headache from it.

454. Another.

Two handfuls of woodruff, two or three oranges cut into slices, two bottles of white wine, and two bottles of claret are put in a bowl; let it infuse an hour, take the herb out, and sweeten to taste.

455. Another.

A handful of woodruff, four sprigs of balm, four to six mint-leaves, as many young strawberry-leaves, and cassis-leaves are put in a bowl; add two lemons cut into slices, freed from peel and seeds, and two or three bottles of Moselle wine; let soak not longer than half an hour, add sugar to taste, and ice, if desired.

(*N. B.* The first one is, to repeat it once more, the simplest and best one.)

456. Militia Bowl.

A beverage similar to Bishop or Cardinal. Infuse the rind of two lemons in one quart of good, white wine six or eight hours; filter the wine, sweeten with half a pound of sugar, put it on ice, and use it when you please.

457. Nectar.

Peel twelve ripe, very fine choice apples; cut into very thin slices; put that in a bowl with the thinly peeled rind of two lemons, cover the slices thickly with powdered sugar, and pour over it a bottle of Rhine or Moselle wine. Cover the bowl, and let it stand from ten to fourteen hours; add, the following day, a bottle of Moselle and one of champagne; put the bowl on ice, and serve.

458. Nectar in the English Style.

(FOR BOTTLING.)

Put the rind of two or three lemons, one pound of raisins (without seeds and cut in pieces), one and a half pounds of loaf-sugar, in a tureen, and pour over it nine quarts of boiling water; after cooling add the juice of the lemons, let the beverage stand a week in a cool place; stir daily, then filter through a flannel bag, and bottle; you may use it right away.

459. Another.

Two pounds of raisins (without seeds and cut in small pieces) and four pounds of sugar are infused in nine quarts of boiling water; stir until the water is getting cool; add two lemons (cut in slices), one and a half to two quarts of rum or best brandy; cover the vessel well and let it stand a week; stir daily a few times, press all through flannel, let it stand for another week for getting clear; decant into bottles for immediate or future use.

460. Orange Bowl.

Rub the peel of one large or two small oranges on sugar; pour over it a bottle of Moselle wine, and let it stand two hours; then peel six oranges very neatly, divide them into nice cuts, remove the seeds and their inner skin, partially, that the juice may flow out freely; add one pound of pulverized sugar and four bottles of white wine; put the bowl on ice, and add, before serving, a bottle of champagne.

461. Orange Cardinal.

Peel an orange very thin with a sharp knife; add three bottles of Rhine wine; let it stand at least from eight to twelve hours; strain the wine through a sieve; add the juice of six oranges and one and a half pounds of sugar.

462. Orgeat.

This is a cooling beverage, especially adapted for sick persons who are forbidden to drink lemonades; but in many cases, as by dancing parties, musical entertainments, etc., also for the healthy, very refreshing and pleasing.

Pour boiling water over one-fourth pound of sweet and eight to ten bitter almonds; place in a sieve; skin them; mash with one-fourth of a pound of sugar, and add, while mashing, a few drops of cold water. Put it in a china pot; add, gradually, one pint of cold water, stir well, and let the mixture stand in a cool place two hours; strain through a cloth; place it on ice; add another quart of cold water and one pony of orange-flower water, and serve.

463. Peach Bowl.

Peel ten to twelve peaches; cut them in quarters; remove the seeds; put that in a bowl; strew thickly with powdered sugar, cover the bowl well, and let it stand from eight to ten hours; add two bottles of Rhine or Moselle wine; place the bowl on ice, and add, finally, a bottle of Seltzer or of champagne.

464. The Pope.

A bowl similar to Bishop or Cardinal, only use Tokay wine instead of red and white wine.

Pare off the rind of two small bitter oranges; put the rind in a bottle of Tokay; cork well, and let stand for twenty-four hours; filter, and sweeten to taste.

465. English Porter Bowl.

Cut three lemons into thin slices; remove the seeds; put the slices in a bowl; pour over it half a pint of sherry and one quart of porter: grate a little nutmeg; place on ice and serve.

466. Bowl à la Parisienne.
(FOR TWELVE.)

A large bowl, containing about two gallons; the juice of six peeled lemons, the juice of six peeled oranges, one pound of pulverized sugar, two quarts of champagne, two quarts of Burgundy; dissolve this exceedingly well; add a bottle of Jamaica rum, half a bottle of brandy, a whiskey-tumbler of chartreuse (green or yellow), three ponies of benedictine, two ponies of curaçao, two ponies of maraschino, one bottle of plain soda, or other mineral water. You may add a small pineapple, peeled and sliced. Mix this well, and have it cold on a large piece of ice; serve in fine glasses.

467. Raspberry Bowl.

The same recipe as for a strawberry bowl, only raspberries in-instead of strawberries.

468. Réséda Bowl.

On a dry, sunny day pluck a little basket of fully developed mignonette blossoms; free them from all green leaves; cut the stalks off to the blossoms, and look carefully that no insects or small caterpillars are on them; then place them in a tureen; infuse them for twelve hours, well covered in half a pint of arrack or brandy and half a bottle of Rhine wine; strain through flannel; add three bottles of Rhine wine; sweeten to taste; put it on ice, and add, before serving, a bottle of champagne or Seltzer.

469. Rum Flip.

Heat three-fourths of a pint of ale; beat three or four eggs with four ounces of pulverized sugar, a teaspoonful of pulverized ginger, a little grated nutmeg and a finely chopped lemon-peel and a gill of old Jamaica rum to a consistent foam; add the nearly boiling ale, while constantly stirring, and pour the beverage a few times from one vessel into another; serve in glasses.

470. Sillabub.

This word is derived from the old English words, "to sile" ("to strain,") "and "bub" ("beverage").

In a large china pot mix one pint of rich, sweet cream, one pint of good Rhine or Hungarian wine, four or five ounces of sugar, on which you have rubbed off the rind of a lemon and the juice of a lemon; let it get very cold on ice; beat to a thick foam, and serve in glasses or cups as dessert, or after coffee.

471. Red Sillabub.

On half a pound of sugar rub the rind of two lemons; break the sugar and dissolve it in a quart of sweet cream; mix three-fourths of a quart of claret and the juice of the lemons with the cream; place on ice for an hour, and serve.

472. Strawberry Bowl.

Take one pint of choice strawberries; cover them with powdered sugar; then take three pints of strawberries and infuse them with one pint of hot sugar syrup two hours; strain them through flannel upon the sugared strawberries; add three or four bottles of Moselle wine; put the bowl on ice, and add, finally, a bottle of champagne.

473. Sweet Bowl.

One pound of powdered sugar, one and a half lemons cut in slices, without the seeds, and one-fourth of an ounce of stick cinnamon, are infused in a bottle of Moselle or Rhine wine twelve hours; strain and serve in glasses.

474. West Indian Sangaree.

Pulverize one-fourth of a pound of loaf-sugar; add one wineglassful of lemon or lime juice; stir well; add a bottle of Madeira, half a pint of good brandy, and one quart of cold water; mix all well, and grate the fourth part of a little nutmeg on top; put in a big lump of ice, and serve with biscuits.

This is a favorite drink in the West Indies, and usually taken cold.

Kaltschalen.

(Bishops.)

Kaltschalen.

475. Apple Bishop.

Peel eighteen to twenty fine, aromatic apples; cut them into thin slices, steam one-third of them with seven ounces of raisins, one glass of Rhine wine, seven ounces of sugar, and the juice of a lemon, and put on ice. The rest of the apple slices are boiled in one and a half quarts of water with some lemon-peel and stick cinnamon to a mash; strain; mix with a bottle of Rhine wine and one pound of pulverized sugar, and serve over the steamed apple slices on plates.

476. Apricot Bishop.

Peel about twelve fine, soft apricots; four of them are cut in pieces and boiled with the skinned seeds (chopped) and with the peel of the apricots and half a pound of sugar; boil half an hour well, strain through a sieve upon the others, which you have cut in two; let all get cold, and add a few glasses of white wine.

477. Beer Bishop.

Pumpernickel is grated on a grater and put in a tureen; mix with it one-fourth of a pound of powdered sugar, one-fourth of a pound of choice raisins, a teaspoonful of powdered cinnamon, an unpeeled lemon, cut in pieces without seeds; add a quart of white beer or lager (*Franziskaner*), and serve.

478. Bilberry Bishop.

Boil two quarts of well-cleaned bilberries with half a pint of water, one-fourth of a pound of sugar, some lemon-peel and some stick cinnamon; strain through a sieve, mix it with two quarts of white wine, cream or milk, place the mixture on ice, and serve over broken Zwieback, grated pumpernickel or snowballs.

479. Cherry Bishop.

Remove the pits of one and a half quarts of fine sour cherries, break one part of the pits, put the cherries and pits with one pint of wine, one and a half quarts of water, six ounces of sugar, some stick cinnamon and lemon-peel in a tureen; let all boil thoroughly until the cherries are perfectly soft; then stir a tablespoonful of corn-starch in cold water, mix that, while continually stirring, to the cherries, let boil a while, strain all through a hair-sieve, and put on ice. When serving, add broken Zwieback, cherries steamed in wine and sugar, snowballs of the beaten whites of eggs, seasoned with lemon sugar, etc.

480. Currant Bishop.

One quart of choice currants are strained through a hair-sieve and mixed with half a pound of powdered sugar and a good quart of light, white wine; put on ice and serve over broken Zwieback or small biscuits.

481. Lemon Bishop.

A bottle of white wine with one quart of water and nine ounces of sugar are heated to the boiling-point (without boiling); add the yolks of six eggs and a spoonful of flour well whipped, and take it from the fire; strain through a sieve, add the peel of two lemons, which you rubbed off on half a pound of sugar, and their juice; mix well and let it get cold in the cellar. When serving, add some biscuits or macaroni.

482. Melon Bishop.

A half or whole very ripe melon is cut into small, cubic pieces; cover them well with sugar, squeeze over it the juice of a lemon and let soak for an hour; add two or three bottles of light, ice-cold white wine; stir thoroughly, add some small biscuits and serve.

483. Mulberry Bishop.

Select from one pint of ripe mulberries the third or fourth part, *i. e.*, the largest and best, place the rest in one or one and a half quarts of water over a slow fire and boil them well; strain, add one pint of wine (best red wine), some lemon-peel and seven ounces of sugar; boil this well together, let it get cold, and serve over the selected berries which you covered with sugar.

484. Orange Bishop.

On half a pound of sugar rub the rind of two oranges; heat to the boiling-point in one pint of water; when the water has got cold, squeeze the juice of four oranges, add one bottle of white wine and the peeled slices of two oranges.

485. Peach Bishop.

Boil a number of peaches cut in two, soft in water after you have removed their pits; mix them with one and a half quarts of white wine and three-fourths of a pound of sugar and let it get cold on ice.

486. Pineapple Bishop.

Peel a pineapple and cut into four pieces; one-half is cut into slices; cover these with sugar and place on ice; grate the other half, boil it up in one quart of sugar syrup and press through a cloth; add to this syrup one and a half bottles of Rhine wine and the juice of a lemon, sweeten to taste with powdered sugar, put wine and slices in a tureen, let it get cold on ice and serve in glasses or on plates.

487. Raspberry Bishop.

From one quart of choice raspberries select the best, cover them with sugar in a tureen, then press the remaining berries through a hair-sieve, mix with one pint of water, one bottle of white wine, the rind of a lemon rubbed off on eight ounces of sugar; pour this mixture over the berries in the tureen, let it get cold on ice and serve with small biscuits.

488. Rice with Wine.

Rub the rind of a lemon on a little over half a pound of sugar; refine this in three-fourths of a quart of water, let it cool, add one bottle of white wine and the juice of two lemons and one-fourth of a pound of rice, slowly boiled before, and place all on ice.

489. Strawberry Bishop.

Put one quart of choice strawberries in a tureen and let it stand with six ounces of powdered sugar an hour; add one quart of white wine, as much of water, and the juice of a lemon; sweeten to taste and grate a little cinnamon on it.

Extra Drinks.

Extra Drinks.

490. Champagne Beer.

Boil in a large, very clean earthen pot five gallons of water with one and a half pounds of sugar—brown rock-candy is the best—until the sugar is completely dissolved; when the water is cool add one and three-fourths ounces of yeast; stir well; cover the pot, and let it stand over night. The following day take off the yeast on the top; place the fluid in a cool place, and decant it into another vessel very carefully; add a stick of cinnamon, and one ounce of lump-sugar, which has been moistened with twelve drops of lemon-oil; let it stand for a couple of hours; bottle and cork well, and put it in the cellar; you may use it after four or five days.

491. Egg Beer.

Place one quart of beer with four ounces of sugar, a stick of cinnamon, and some pieces of lemon-peel in a pot over the fire, and heat it to boiling; meanwhile beat six whole fresh eggs to foam, and add the boiling beer, while continually stirring; then serve it in cups.

492. Ginger Beer.

Put in a large earthen vessel the rind of a thinly peeled lemon and the juice of four, two ounces of pulverized ginger, two and one-half pounds of powdered sugar, half an ounce of cremor tartari; pour over it ten quarts of boiling water, and add, after the water is lukewarm only, one ounce of pressed yeast, dissolved in a little water; stir the fluid well, and let it ferment to the following day. Then take off the yeast on top; decant the beer carefully into bottles, so as not to disturb the yeast; cork well, and the beer is ready for use after three or four days.

493. Ginger Pop.

Put one pound of lump-sugar, one ounce of pulverized ginger, one ounce of cremor tartari in five quarts of boiling water; when the water is nearly cold, add one ounce of pressed yeast, dissolved in a little water; strain it into bottles; tie the cork with wire, and you may use the beverage after six or eight hours.

494. Gloria.

The French are very fond of this beverage.

Take very strong, well-strained coffee, and pour it over half a cupful of sugar; the result will be a consistent syrup; in the moment of serving pour in a teaspoonful of brandy; light it, and extinguish the flame after a few seconds, and drink the gloria as hot as you possibly can.

495. Kvass.

This, for every Russian household, necessary national beverage, which is also used for different soups and other dishes, is manufactured for the family use in the following way:

Ten pounds of rye flour, one pound of malt, and one pound of buckwheat flour are stirred in a tub with three quarts of warm water; then pour over it three quarts of boiling water; after half an hour add again six quarts of boiling water, and repeat this in half-hourly intervals three times more; stir the flour in the water well; let it get cool, cover, and let it stand in a rather warm place; the following day you thin the kvass with cold water; put it in a cool place; let it thoroughly sour, and bottle. When the kvass is nearly used up, leave a couple of quarts of the beverage in the tub for the next souring; the thick sediment at the bottom is then thrown away, but it may be used on farms successfully as food for the beasts of burden.

Another recipe is the following:

Twenty pounds of rye flour, and as much malt flour are stirred with cold water, and kneaded well; then form loaves of bread from ten to twelve pounds each; press with the fingers some deep holes into them; pour cold water into these holes; place the loaves in a very hot baking-oven, and bake them brownish black; leave them over night in the oven; break forty pounds to moderate-sized pieces; put them in a tub; pour fifty to sixty quarts of boiling water over them; cover the pot with canton flannel and a wooden lid very well, and let soak for two hours. Pour the entire quantity into a cask, the bottom of which is covered with cross-laid slats, which again are covered by straw to prevent the falling through of the bread; through a side-faucet decant the kvass, and fill it again into the cask; repeat this a few times to clear it sufficiently; in a vessel already soured it need stay for only twenty-four hours, but in a new cask it must stand for a few days until it is sufficiently sour.

Besides this bread-kvass, this beverage may be made also from fruits: so you may make apple-kvass by rowing apple-slices and whole pears on strings, and drying them in the sun; in a cask of about fifteen gallons you put twenty-four quarts of dried apples, and as many dried pears, and fill the cask with boiled but cooled-off water; let it stand for three days on a rather warm place; then bring it into the cellar; cover the bung-hole with canvas, and let the kvass ferment. After fermentation bung the cask; bottle after four weeks; add to each bottle a handful of raisins; cork, and seal, and let them lie a few months in a cellar; cover them with a layer of sand.

Fruit Wines.

Fruit Wines.

496. English Apricot Wine.

Boil twelve pounds of ripe, stoneless apricots with one pound of lump-sugar, half an hour, in twelve quarts of water; add one-fourth of the peeled and roughly mashed kernels, and let the fluid get cool in a well-covered vessel. After cooling, add, while stirring, a tablespoonful of beer-yeast; let it ferment three or four days. Then fill the juice into a very well-cleaned cask, and add, when the fermentation is complete, a bottle of Rhine wine; let the cask rest for half a year, fill the contents into bottles, and let them lie a year before using.

497. Bilberry Wine.

Boil three pints of water with four quarts of selected bilberries for twenty minutes, strain the juice through canton flannel, cover, and let it stand for half an hour; then fill it carefully into another pot; let it boil once more a few seconds with twelve ounces of sugar, one-eighth of an ounce of ground cinnamon, and one-tenth of an ounce of ground cloves; bottle after cooling, seal the bottles, and put them in the cellar.

498. English Blackberry Wine.

Put any large quantity of ripe and dry blackberries in a large stone jar, pour over it boiling water, and place it over night in a tepid oven; squeeze the berries thoroughly in the morning, strain through a fine sieve. and let the juice ferment a fortnight; then add to each four quarts of juice one pound of pulverized sugar, and half a pint of brandy or rum; fill the fluid into a cask, bung well, and let it lie in a cellar a few months before using.

499. Cider.

Cider is chiefly produced in large quantities by pressing apples with an addition of water; yet one may obtain smaller quantities for the family use without too great trouble, by grating fine, juicy peeled apples on a grater; filter the juice through a cloth, pour it into stone jars, and add some roasted apples to hasten fermentation. When, after a couple of days, a skin appears on the juice, fermentation is complete; remove the skin, bottle the cider, and keep it in a cool place.

Larger quantities of cider are obtained by mashing good, juicy apples; press them, and fill the juice into a small Rhine wine cask. Place this cask in a cool room upon a skid, when the juice will soon begin to ferment; fermentation will take about a fortnight; during this time remove with a clean piece of linen all stuffs thrown to the surface; as soon as fermentation is done fill the cask up with water, bung it well, and let it lie in the cellar half a year; decant it into another cask, let it lie for another two months, and fill into bottles.

500. Currant Wine.

Collect the perfectly ripe currants on a sunny day, clean, and put them in a big earthen or wooden pot, and mash them with a wooden masher; let ferment in a cellar, and strain through a hair-sieve with a wooden spoon; never use your hands; decant into a little cask; add to each quart of juice half a pound of powdered sugar, and to each twelve quarts of juice one quart of brandy or arrack; let the wine stand six weeks, bottle, and use after two months.

501. Currant Wine in the English Style.

From twelve to fourteen quarts of currants are mashed, the juice pressed out, and the remnants covered with eighteen quarts of cold water; stir repeatedly, press out again the following day, mix with the juice, and fourteen pounds of loaf-sugar; when the sugar is dissolved, fill the juice into a cask, so as not to fill it entirely; bung, and bore a small hole with a gimlet; let it stand four weeks in a place where the temperature never sinks below 68° F.

After this period add three pounds of sugar dissolved in two quarts of warm water; shake the cask well, and bung again. Six or eight weeks later, when no more noise of the fermentation can be heard going on, decant, add two quarts of brandy; let the wine stand two months in the cellar; then fill into another, but not new cask, which must be entirely filled, and bung. After three or four years, always in a temperature not below 68° F., bottle, and you obtain a delicious beverage, which much resembles good grape wine.

502. English Dandelion Wine.

Pluck about four quarts of the yellow petals of the dandelion blossoms; take care that they are clean from insects; infuse them three days in four and a half quarts of hot water; stir it now and then, strain through flannel, and boil the water half an hour with the rind of a lemon and of an orange, some ginger, and three and a half pounds of lump-sugar; after boiling add the lemon and orange, cut into slices, without seeds; let it get cool; add a little yeast on toast. After one or two days the fermentation is done; then fill into a cask and after two months you may bottle.

(The wine is very good against liver-complaints.)

503. Elder Wine.

Twenty-six pounds of elderberries are boiled in fifty quarts of water, an hour, while adding one ounce of pimento and two ounces of ginger; place forty-four pounds of sugar in a tub, strain the fluid over it, squeeze all the juice out of the berries, add four ounces of cremor tartari; let the fluid stand two days, fill into a cask, place a brick over the bung-hole, and stir every other day.

When fermentation is complete, add two or three quarts of cognac spirits; bung, and bottle after four months.

504. Ginger Wine.

Boil sixteen pounds of sugar and twelve ounces of well-pulverized Jamaica ginger in twenty-four quarts of water half an hour; skim carefully, and let it stand till the following day.

Cut seven pounds of raisins in pieces, remove the seeds, put the raisins in a cask with four quarts of good brandy or arrack, and three or four lemons, sliced and without seeds; pour over it the fluid, which you decant carefully; bung the cask; clear the wine after a fortnight with one ounce of pale white glue, and bottle after another fortnight.

505. Gooseberry Wine.

Unripe, but otherwise perfectly developed gooseberries of a good kind are mashed in a tub; after twenty-four hours decant the juice; infuse the berries in lukewarm water twelve hours in the proportion of one quart of water to four quarts of berries; strain; mix it with the decanted juice; add to each twenty quarts of fluid twelve pounds of broken sugar, and let the wine ferment in a warm place. After two or three days fill into a cask; add to each twenty quarts of wine two quarts of best brandy; bung well, and place it in not too cold a cellar; to obtain an excellent gooseberry wine it ought to remain in the cellar five years, yet you may decant after a year: of course the product will be inferior.

506. Sparkling Gooseberry Wine.

Forty pounds of large, but still green gooseberries are mashed in a tub, infused in eighteen quarts of lukewarm water; stir thoroughly; decant the water, and squeeze the fruits through a sieve, while you mix it again with four or five quarts of water.

Dissolve thirty pounds of loaf-sugar, and three and one-third ounces of cremor tartari in the juice, and add water to have altogether fifty quarts of fluid; cover the tub with a cloth, and let it stand undisturbed two days in a temperature not below 60° F.

Then pour the wine into a cask containing exactly 45 or 46 quarts, and keep the remaining fluid for the purpose of filling up afterward during fermentation; when you can no longer hear the hissing noise of fermentation, bung, but make a hole beside the bung with a gimlet, closed by a small cork, which is to be taken out every other day to avoid bursting. After ten or twelve days cork solidly; place the cask in a cool cellar, and let it lie till the end of December; decant the wine into a new cask, and clear with pale white glue in the proportion of one ounce to one quart of wine.

In spring bottle at the time when the gooseberries of the same kind begin to bloom; fasten your corks with wire.

507. Honey Wine à la Russe.

Refine four pounds of honey, and mix it with two pounds of pulverized sugar, the rind of four lemons rubbed on sugar, and the juice of six lemons; after cooling mix it well with eight quarts of cold well-water; pour the fluid into a cask, bung it, and put it in the cellar. After a fortnight decant, bottle, cork, and seal, and let the bottles lie a few weeks before using.

508. Lemon Wine.

Boil six quarts of water with four pounds of lump-sugar to the consistency of syrup; peel five lemons, and put the rind in a large, clean pot; pour the boiling syrup over the rind; when the syrup is cool add the juice of ten lemons, a piece of toast covered with a spoonful of yeast, and let it stand two days, when fermentation begins. Then remove the rind; pour the fluid into a cask which must be completely filled; let the wine ferment, and cork when the fermentation is complete. After three months bottle and use.

509. Orange Wine.

Boil twenty-eight pounds of loaf-sugar in thirty-two quarts of water, with the whites and the cracked shells of four eggs, the whites being beaten to foam; skim well; let the concoction get cool; add the juice of ninety bitter oranges; mix all very well; filter; add half a pound of yeast put on toast, let stand for twenty-four hours; fill into a cask, add one quart of fine brandy. After fermentation is complete, bung well; after three months decant into another cask, add another quart of brandy, let it lie for a year, bottle, and let the bottles lie for three months before using.

510. Pear Champagne.

Juicy and sweet pears are mashed; press the juice out, and fill it into a small cask; cover the bung-hole with a piece of muslin, and let it stand for a few days. The juice begins now to ferment, and to foam considerably; after the fermentation is complete fill into another cask, bung well, and let it lie in a cellar for six weeks; after this fill the wine into bottles, fasten the corks with wire, and you may use it after three or four more weeks.

511. Raisin Wine.

Pour twenty-four quarts of boiling water over twenty-four pounds of extra good raisins; add six pounds of sugar; let it stand a fortnight; stir daily; decant the fluid, squeeze the raisins, and add three-fourths of a pound of finely pulverized cremor tartari; fill into a cask, let it ferment; bung; let it lie for six months, decant into another cask; let it lie again three months, and bottle.

512. Another.

If you wish a raisin wine resembling in taste the muscatel wine you proceed as follows:

Boil eight pounds of choice raisins in twenty-four quarts of water perfectly soft, press them through a sieve, add the mass to the water in which the raisins have been boiled, likewise add twelve pounds of lump-sugar; when the sugar is dissolved let the wine ferment in a cask by adding one-fourth of a quart of yeast. When the fermentation is nearly over, hang a linen bag filled with two and a half quarts of elderberries into the cask; remove the bag as soon as the wine has the required taste; let the wine lie for six months and bottle.

513. Raisin Wine in the Hebrew Style.

The raisin wine, which is used as so-called Easter wine during the Passover in all orthodox Hebrew families, is easily made as follows:

A fortnight before the feast, select three pounds of fine raisins; cut them in small pieces and remove the seeds; put them with one pound of sugar in a jug and pour over six or seven quarts of cold water; place the vessel, covered, on or behind the hearth; skim after three or four days; filter through a funnel lined with linen or blotting-paper into bottles; add to each bottle some stick cinnamon, lemon-peel, and cloves; cork well and put them in the cellar, until you use them.

514. Raspberry Wine.

Ripe raspberries are mashed with a wooden spoon and put into a stone jar; add one quart of cold water to each quart of berries. The following day you decant the fluid, press the berries through a cloth, add one pound of sugar to every quart of wine; fill the wine into a cask and stir daily; when fermentation is done, add one quart of white wine to every four quarts of raspberry wine; bung the barrel, let it lie three months, bottle the wine and it is ready for use.

515. English Raspberry Wine.

Throw twenty quarts of ripe raspberries into a tub, pour twenty quarts of boiling water over them, cover the tub well and let it stand until the following day; skim, press the berries through a hair-sieve and let the fluid stand again from four to five hours. Decant it into a barrel, add gradually twelve pounds of pulverized sugar, mix one quart of the fluid with three tablespoonfuls of very fresh ale yeast and mix this with the rest of the wine; cover the bung-hole with a piece of paper and a brickstone and let the wine ferment. As soon as the fermentation is over, bung the barrel well, and after four weeks decant the wine into another clean barrel; clear the fluid with two-thirds of an ounce of pale, sweet glue and add one quart of fine brandy to the wine; bung well and let it lie for a year in a cool cellar; bottle and seal, and let the bottles lie for another year.

516. Sloe Wine.

Fresh, ripe sloes are put in a tub, for each quart of sloes one quart of water; boil the water and pour it boiling over the sloes; let that stand five days; stir daily. Add to each quart of fluid one pound of loaf-sugar; dissolve by continually stirring; fill all in a cask, add one pint of brandy to each six quarts of fluid; let it lie in the cask for a year, at least, before bottling; let the bottles lie for another year, when the wine will have the goût of port wine.

517. Spiced Wine.

Wash one-fourth of an ounce of cloves, as much ginger, twice as much cinnamon and nutmeg; pour over it ten or twelve quarts of Madeira and let it stand for a few days in moderate warmth; strain it through blotting-paper and drink it in very small doses.

518. Strawberry Wine.

Pour over twelve quarts of strawberries twelve quarts of cold water and let stand twenty-four hours. Strain, add eight pounds of sugar, eight quarts of apple cider, the thin peel of a lemon and one ounce of cremor tartari; fill all in a barrel; it must occupy not more than three-fourths of the barrel's volume; bung, and bore a hole beside the bung with a gimlet; let the barrel stand four weeks on a temperate place. Then add three pounds of sugar, shake the barrel well and bung again. After six to eight weeks decant, add one quart of cognac, fill back the wine into the cleaned barrel, place it two months in the cellar; after this time decant into a smaller cask, which must be filled entirely; bung well; bottle after three years and use.

519. Wischniak.

(CHERRY WINE WITH HONEY À LA RUSSE.)

Into a strong little cask, well bound with iron bands, you fill ripe sour cherries, so that only about two inches room is left; then pour slowly over the cherries clean, white, unboiled honey containing no particles of wax, and fill each empty space between the cherries with honey. As soon as the upper layer of cherries is nearly covered by honey, put the cover tightly on the cask, bung and seal well bung-hole and lid, or best cover the entire surface with pitch to prevent any air from entering; then sink the cask in sand or earth for three months; during this time the fermentation is going on; there is great danger the cask might burst, unless it be of very strong material. After three months the wine is filtered, bottled, and is ready for use.

Poetry.

Poetry.

Thirsty earth drinks up the rain,
Trees from earth drink that again;
Ocean drinks the air; the sun
Drinks the sea, and him the moon.
Any reason, canst thou think,
I should thirst while all these drink?

Anacreon.

Drink! enjoy the hour; what the morrow bringeth
  None can tell; then vex not thy soul with idle care;
Being and Not-being but a point divideth;
  Life is but a moment; then make that moment fair.
Piles of hoarded treasure, heaps of gold and silver—
  Hades self might chuckle, when thou call'st them thine;
Surely thou hast nothing but that which thou enjoyest:
  Only while enjoying canst thou say, " 'Tis mine."

An Old Poet.

He who joy has never found
In the flute's entrancing sound,
Bacchus' gifts who dares despise
Song and laugh and maidens' eyes;
He who at his grudging board,
Thinks upon his growing hoard,
Reckoning interest in his head—
Him I count already dead.
Shuddering and disgusted, I
Pass the meagre carcass by.

An Old Poet.

Now with roses we are crowned,
Let our mirth and cups go round,
While a girl, whose hand a spear,
Wound with ivy twines, does bear,
With her white feet beats the ground
To the lyre's harmonious sound,
Played by some fairy boy, whose choice
Skill is heightened by his voice;
Bright-haired Love, with his divine
Mother, and the god of wine
Will flock hither, glad to see
Old men of their company.

ANACREON.

Othello, II. 3.

AND let me the canakin clink, clink,
And let me the canakin clink:
    A soldier's a man,
    A life's but a span,
Why, then, let a soldier drink.

Antony and Cleopatra, II. 7.

COME, thou monarch of the vine,
Plumpy Bacchus, with pink eyne:
In thy vats our cares be drown'd;
With thy grapes our hairs be crown'd;
Cup us, till the world go round;
Cup us, till the world go round.

King Henry IV., Second Part, IV. 3.

A GOOD sherris-sack hath a twofold operation in it: it ascends me into the brain, dries me there all the foolish, and dull and crudy vapours which environ it, makes it apprehensive, quick, forgetive, full of nimble, fiery, and delectable shapes, which delivered o'er to the voice (the tongue), which is the birth, becomes excellent wit. The second property of your excellent sherris is, the warming of the blood, which, before cold and settled, left the liver white and pale, which is the badge of pusillanimity and cowardice; but the sherris warms it, and makes it course from the inwards to the parts extreme. It illumines the face, which, as a beacon, gives warning to all the rest of this little kingdom, man, to arm; and then the vital commoners, and inland petty spirits muster me all to their captain, the heart; who, great and puffed up with this retinue, does any deed of courage; and this valor comes of sherris. So that skill in the weapon is nothing without sack, for that sets it a-work; and learning, a mere hoard of gold kept by a devil, till sack commences it, and sets it in act and use. Hereof comes it that Prince Harry is valiant, for the cold blood he did naturally inherit of his father, he has, like lean, steril, and bare land, manured, husbanded, and tilled with excellent endeavour of drinking good, and good store of fertile sherris, that he has become very hot and valiant. If I had a thousand sons, the first human principle I would teach them should be, to forswear their potations, and to addict themselves to sack.

Scotch Drink.

BY ROBERT BURNS.

Let other poets raise a fracas
'Bout vines, an' wines, an' druken Bacchus
An' crabbit names an' stories wrack us,
   An' grate our lug,
I sing the juice Scotch bear can mak' us,
   In glass or jug.

O thou, my muse! guid auld Scotch drink,
Whether thro' wimplin' worms thou jink,
Or, richly brown, ream o'er the brink
   In glorious faem,
Inspire me, till I lisp an' wink,
   To sing thy name.

Let husky wheat the haughs adorn,
An' aits set up their awnie horn,
An' pease an' beans, at e'en or morn,
   Perfume the plain,
Leeze me on thee, John Barleycorn,
   Thou king o' grain !

On thee aft Scotland chows her cood,
In souple scones, the wale o' food !
Or tumblin' in the boilin' flood,
   Wi' kail an' beef;
But when thou pours thy strong heart's blood,
   There thou shines chief.

Food fills the wame, an' keeps us livin';
Tho' life's a gift no worth receivin',
When heavy-dragg'd wi' pine an' grievin';
   But, oil'd by thee,
The wheels o' life gae down hill scrievin',
   Wi' rattlin' glee.

Thou clears the head o' doited Lear,
Thou cheers the heart o' drooping Care;
Thou strings the nerves o' Labour sair
   At 's weary toil;
Thou ev'n brightens dark Despair
   Wi' gloomy smile.

Aft, clad in massy, siller weed,
Wi' gentles thou erects thy head:
Yet humbly kind in time o' need,
   The poor man's wine,
His wee drap praritch, or his bread
   Thou kitchens fine.

Thou art the life o' public haunts;
But thee what were our fairs an' rants !
E'en godly meetings o' the saunts
   By thee inspir'd,
When gaping they besiege the tents
   Are doubly fir'd.

That merry night we get the corn in,
O sweetly then thou reams the horn in!
Or reckin', on a New-Year mornin',
        In cog or bicker,
An' just a wee drap sp'ritual burn in
        An' gusty sucker!

When Vulcan gies his bellows breath,
An' ploughmen gather wi' their graith,
O rare! to see thee fizz an' freath
        I' th' lugget caup!
Then Burnewin comes on like Death
        At ev'ry chap.

Nae mercy, then, for airn or steel,
The brawnie, bainie ploughman chiel,
Brings hard owrehip, wi' sturdy wheel,
        The strong forehammer,
Till block an' studdie ring an' reel
        Wi' dinsome clamour.

When skirlin' weanies see the light,
Thou makes the gossips clatter bright,
How fumblin' cuifs their dearies slight
        Wae worth the name!
Nae howdie gets a social night,
        Or plack frae them.

When neebors anger at a plea,
An' just as wud as wud can be,
How easy can the barley-bree
        Cement the quarrel!
It's aye the cheapest lawyer's fee
        To taste the barrel.

Alake! that e'er my muse has reason
To wyte her countrymen wi' treason!
But monie daily weet their weason
        Wi' liquors nice;
An' hardly, in a winter's season,
        E'er spier her price.

Wae worth that brandy, burning trash !
Fell source o' monie a pain an' brash !
Turns monie a poor, doylt, druken hash
   O' half his days;
An' sends, beside, auld Scotland's cash
   To her warst faes.

Ye Scots, who wish auld Scotland well,
Ye chief, to you my tale I tell,
Poor plackless devils, like mysel,
   It sets you ill,
Wi' bitter, dearthfu' wines to mell,
   Or foreign gill.

May gravels round his blather wrench,
An' gouts torment him inch by inch,
Wha twists his gruntle wi' a glunch
   O' sour disdain,
Out owre a glass o' whiskey punch
   Wi' honest men.

O whiskey ! soul o' plays an' pranks
Accept a Bardie's gratefu' thanks !
When wantin' thee, what tuneless cranks
   Are my poor verses !
Thou comes—they rattle i' their ranks
   At ither's a——s !

Thee Fernitosh ! O sadly lost !
Scotland lament frae coast to coast !
Now colic grips an' barkin' hoast,
   May kill us a',
For loyal Forbes's charter'd boast
   Is ta'en awa !

Thou curst horse-leeches o' th' Excise
Wha mak' the whiskey stells their prize !
Haud up thy han', Deil ! ance, twice, thrice !
   There, seize the blinkers !
An' bake them up in brunstane pies
   For poor d——d drinkers.

Fortune ! if thou'll but gie me still
Hale breeks, a scone, an' whiskey gill,
An' rowth o' rhyme, to rave at will,
   Tak' a' the rest,
An' deal't about as thy blind skill
   Directs thee best.

The Cure for All Care.

BY ROBERT BURNS.

No churchman am I, for to rail and to write,
No statesman nor soldier, to plot or to fight;
No sly man of business, contriving to snare—
For a big-bellied bottle's the whole of my care.

The peer I don't envy; I give him his bow;
I scorn not the peasant, tho' ever so slow;
But a club of good fellows, like those that are here,
And a bottle like this are my glory and care.

Here passes the squire, on his brother—his horse;
There, centum per centum, the cit with his purse;
But see you The Crown, how it waves in the air !
There a big-bellied bottle still eases my care.

The wife of my bosom, alas ! she did die;
For sweet consolation to church I did fly;
I found that old Solomon proved it fair,
That a big-bellied bottle's a cure for all care.

I once was persuaded a venture to make;
A letter informed me that all was a wreck;
But the pursy old landlord just waddled up-stairs
With a glorious bottle that ended my cares.

"Life's cares they are comforts," a maxim laid down
By the bard, what d'ye call him? that wore the black gown;
And faith, I agree with th' old prig to a hair;
For a big-bellied bottle's a haven of care.

Then, fill up a bumper, and make it o'erflow,
The honours masonic prepare for the throw;
May every true brother of the compass and square
Have a big-bellied bottle when harass'd with care.

Antwort Eines Trunkenen Dichters.

GOTTHOLD EPHRAIM LESSING.

EIN trunk'ner Dichter leerte
   Sein Glas auf jeden Zug;
Ihn warnte sein Gefaehrte:
   "Hoer auf! Du hast genug."
Bereit vom Stuhl zu sinken,
   Sprach der: "Du bist nicht klug;
Zu viel kann man wohl trinken,
   Doch nie trinkt man genug."

Die Staerke des Weines.

GOTTHOLD EPHRAIM LESSING.

WEIN ist staerker als das Wasser;
Dies gesteh'n auch seine Hasser.
Wasser reisst wohl Eichen um,
   Und hat Haeuser umgerissen;
Und ihr wundert euch darum,
   Dass der Wein mich umgerissen?

Der Alte und der Junge Wein.

GOTTHOLD EPHRAIM LESSING.

IHR Alten trinkt, Euch jung und froh zu trinken,
   Drum mag der junge Wein
   Fuer Euch, Ihr Alten, sein.
Der Juengling trinkt, sich alt und klug zu trinken.
   Drum muss der alte Wein
   Fuer mich den Juengling sein.

An den Wein.

GOTTHOLD EPHRAIM LESSING.

WEIN, wenn ich dich jetzo trinke,
Wenn ich dich als Juengling trinke,
    Sollst du mich in allen Sachen
Dreist und klug, beherzt und weise,
Mir zum Nutz' und dir zum Preise;
    Kurz, zu einem Alten machen.

Wein, wenn ich dich kuenftig trinke,
Werd' ich dich als Alter trinken,
    Sollst du mich geneigt zum Lachen,
Unbesorgt fuer Tod und Luegen,
Dir zum Ruhm, mir zum Vergnuegen,
    Kurz, zu einem Juengling machen.

Dithyrambe.

FRIEDRICH VON SCHILLER.

NIMMER, das glaubt mir, nimmer erscheinen die Goetter,
    Nimmer allein.
Kaum dass ich Bacchus, den Lustigen, habe,
Kommt auch schon Amor, der laechelnde Knabe,
    Phœbus, der Herrliche, findet sich ein.
Sie nahen, sie kommen, die Himmlischen alle,
Mit Goettern erfuellt sich die irdische Halle.

Sagt, wie bewirt' ich, der Erdgebor'ne,
    Himmlischen Chor?
Schenket mir euer unsterbliches Leben,
Goetter! was kann euch der Sterbliche geben?
    Hebet zu eurem Olymp mich empor!
Die Freude, sie wohnt nur in Jupiter's Saale;
O fuellet mit Nectar, o reicht mir die Schale!

Reich' ihm die Schale! Schenke dem Dichter,
    Hebe, nur ein!
Netz' ihm die Augen mit himmlischem Thaue,
Dass er den Styx, den verhassten, nicht schaue,
    Einer der Unsern sich duenke zu sein.
Sie rauschet, sie perlet die himmlische Quelle,
Der Busen wird ruhig, das Auge wird helle.

Punschlied.

FRIEDRICH VON SCHILLER.

VIER Elemente,
  Innig gesellt,
Bilden das Leben,
  Bauen die Welt.

Presst der Citrone
  Saftigen Stern!
Herb ist des Lebens
  Innerster Kern.

Jetzt mit des Zuckers
  Linderndem Saft
Zaehmet die herbe
  Brennende Kraft!

Giesset des Wassers
  Sprudelnden Schwall!
Wasser umfaenget
  Ruhig das All.

Tropfen des Geistes
  Giesset hinein!
Leben dem Leben
  Gibt er allein.

Eh' es verduftet,
  Schoepfet es schnell!
Nur wenn er gluehet,
  Labet der Quell.

Die stille Freude wollt ihr stoeren?
　Lasst mich bei meinem Becher Wein!
Mit andern kann man sich belehren,
　Begeistert wird man nur allein.

　　　　　JOHANN WOLFGANG VON GOETHE.

Aus dem Feuerquell des Weines,
　Aus dem Zaubergrund des Bechers
　　Sprudelt Gift und suesse Labung;
Sprudelt Schoenes und Gemeines:
　Nach dem eig'nen Wert des Zechers,
　　Nach des Trinkenden Begabung.

In Gemeinheit tief versunken
　Liegt der Thor, vom Rausch bemeistert;
Wenn *er* trinkt—wird er betrunken,
　Trinken *wir*—sind wir begeistert!
Spruehen hohe Witzesfunken,
　Reden, wie mit Engelszungen,
Und von Gluth sind wir durchdrungen,
　Und von Schoenheit sind wir trunken!

Denn es gleicht der Wein dem Regen,
　Der im Schmutze selbst zu Schmutz wird,
Doch auf gutem Acker Segen
　Bringt, und jedermann zu Nutz wird.

　　　　　FRIEDRICH BODENSTEDT.

Weinlied.

OTTO ROQUETTE.

Das war zu Assmannshausen
　Wohl an dem kuehlen Rhein,
Da zog ich frisch und wohlgemuth
　Zum alten Thor hinein.
　　　Zu Assmannshausen waechst ein Wein,
　　　　Ich meint', das muesst' der Beste sein,
　　Der Assmannshaeuser Wein.

Und als ich kam zum Niederwald,
  Da sah ich Ruedesheim,
Da war's so lustig und so schoen,
  Ich meint', ich waer' daheim.
    Zu Ruedesheim, da waechst ein Wein,
    Ich meint', das muesst' der Beste sein,
  Der Wein von Ruedesheim.

Und weiter ging's nach Geisenheim,
  Da baut'ich Huetten gern.
Doch schon erglaenzt Johannisberg—
  O aller Sterne Stern!
    Ja troeste dich, du armer Wicht,
    Johannisberger schenkt man nicht,
  Als nur besternten Herrn.

Nun sagt mir eins, ist das wohl recht
  Von dem besternten Tross,
Dass er den allerbesten Wein
  Dem durst'gen Mund verschloss?
    Das Beste, das im Lande waechst,
    Verschliessen, gleich als waer's verhext—
  Ei, was mich das verdross!

Und gebt ihr nicht das Beste gleich,
  Das Gute bleibt uns noch,
Die bess're Sorte zoegert nicht,
  Das Beste kommt uns doch.
    Drum trinket, bis kein Tropfen mehr,
    Zuletzt muss doch das Beste her,
  Durst sprengt des Fasses Joch!

TRINKT Wein! das ist mein alter Spruch,
Und wird auch stets mein neuer sein;
Kauft euch der Flasche Weisheitsbuch,
  Und sollt es noch so theuer sein!

Als Gott der Herr die Welt erschuf,
Sprach er: der Mensch sei Koenig hier!

Es soll des Menschen Haupt voll Witz,
    Es soll sein Trank voll Feuer sein!

Dies ist der Grund, dass Adam bald
Vom Paradies vertrieben ward:
Er floh den Wein, d'rum konnt' es ihm
    In Eden nicht geheuer sein!

Die ganze Menschheit ward vertilgt,
Nur Noah blieb mit seinem Haus,
Der Herr sprach: weil Du Wein gebaut,
    Sollst Du mein Knecht, mein treuer sein.

Die Wassertrinker seien jetzt
Ersaeuft im Wasser allzumal,
Nur Du, mein Knecht, sollst aufbewahrt
    Im hoelzernen Gemaeuer sein!

Mirza-Schaffy! Dir ward die Wahl
In diesem Falle nicht zur Qual;
Du hast den Wein erkuert, willst nie
    Ein Wasserungeheuer sein!

FRIEDRICH BODENSTEDT.

Index.

(The Figures Indicate the Number of the Drink.)

A

Absinthe	228
à la Parisienne	105
aux Dieux	106
frappé, American style	104
Cocktail	8
Admiral	317
Admiral, The Great	107
Alabazam	108
Ale Flip	318
Punch	319
Alliance de Neufchâtel	320
Almonds' Essence	229
Alymeth	321
Ananas Bowl	432
Cordial	230, 433
Julep	434
Punch	323
à l' Amérique	324
Angelica Cordial	231
Angelus, The	9
Anisette Cordial	232
Anticipation	10
Appetit, L'	109
Appetizer, The Great	12
à l' Italienne	14
Apple Bishop	475
Blossom	110
Bowl	435
Brandy	316
Toddy, hot	33
Après Souper	111
Apricot Bishop	476
Cordial	233
Sherbet	62
Wine, English	496
Arc de Triomphe, L'	114

Arrack	234
Foam	325
Punch	326, 327
Aurore, L'	15
Avant Déjeuner	113
Avant Souper	112

B

Badminton	436
Balm Cordial	235
Baseball Lemonade	51
Basle Kirschwasser	236
Bavaroise à l'eau	52
au chocolat	63
à l'Italienne	64
au Lait	65
Mexicaine	53
Beef Tea, hot	34
Beer Bishop	477
Bowl, English	437
Chaudeau	329
Grog	330
Punch	328
Beginner, The	16
Benedictine	238
Benefactor, hot	35
Bilberry Bishop	478
Cordial	237
Lemonade	66
Wine	497
Bishop Cordial	239
Cold	438
English, warm	439
Russian	440
Bitter Orange Cordial	240, 241
Bitter Sweet Cocktail	11
Black Rose	46

INDEX.

Blackberry Wine, English.. 498
Blue Blazer, The Old Style. 36
Bon-Appetit 13
Bon Boire, Le............. 117
Bowl à la Parisienne....... 466
Brahmapootra............. 118
Brain-Duster, The......... 17
Brandy, Hot.............. 37
    Crusta................ 119
    Punch, English........ 331
    Rose 120
    Toddy................ 121
Bridge Bracer, The........ 122
Bristol Punch 332
Broker's Thought, The 123
Bunch of Violets........... 223

C

Calla Lily................. 125
Campichello Punch 335
Cardinal 441, 442, 443
Cassis Liqueur............ 242
    Ratafia............... 243
Catawba Cobbler 91
Celery Bowl à l'Amérique.. 444
Champagne Beer.......... 490
    Bowl................. 447
    Cobbler............... 92
    Crême................ 337
    Cup 130
    Punch 336
Chartreuse................ 244
Chat, The................. 338
Cherry Bishop 479
    Brandy, English...247, 248
    Cordial à la Française
      245 246
    Essence, wild.......... 314
    Lemonade 67
      (for the sick)...... 68
    Ratafia.......249, 250, 251
    Sherbet............... 69
Chocolate Punch 127
Christophlet 252
Cider..................... 499
    Bowl, English.....445, 446
Cinnamon Cordial 253
Citronelle................. 70
Claret Bowl, English 449
    Cobbler............... 94
    Cup 128

Claret Punch..........126, 341
    cold 340
    English 339
Clove Cordial 254
Club Cocktail 29
Coffee and Rum 132
Coffee Liqueur 255
Cognac 256
Columbus Punch 131
Confession of Love 342
Correspondent, The 133
Cosmopolitan Cooler, The.. 129
Crambambuli 343
Cream Fizz 101
Cream Punch à l'Amérique. 344
Crown, The............... 136
Curaçao 257
    Punch 137
Currant Bishop............ 480
    Lemonade............ 71
    Metheglin............. 259
    Ratafia............... 258
    Shrub 345
    Wine 500
      in the English Style 501

D

Dandelion Wine, English... 502
Delicious Sour, The 4
Duplex, The 140

E

Easter Crocus............. 134
Egg Beer.............115, 491
    Grog 346
    Liquor................ 348
    Milk Punch 349
    Nogg................. 142
      General Harrison's. 141
    Punch 350
    Punch............347, 351
      cold 352
    Wine 354, 355
      cold 353
Elder Brandy, English..... 260
    Wine 503
Encore 145
English Ratafia, Red....... 261
"Evening Sun, The " 217
Exquisite 18
Eye-Opener 143

F

Fancy Hot Sherry	48
Fig Sherbet	73
Fin du Siècle, La	147
First One, The	19
Fletsch	359
Flip	360
Forget-me-not	150
Foundation, The	144
Frappé à la Guillaume	151
French Ratafia aux Quatre Fruits	262, 263
Fruit Frappé	153
Punch	361

G

Gem, The	157
George IV. Punch	362
Gilmore Punch	160
Gin	264
Bowl, English	450
Fizz, Plain	95
Puff	159
Punch	365
Ginger Beer	492
Cordial	265
Pop	493
Wine	504
Gingerette	266
Giroflée	366
Gladstone, The	20
Glasgow Punch	367
Gloria	494
Glorious Fourth, The	161
Golden Fizz	97
Gooseberry Lemonade	74
Wine	505
Sparkling	506
Grand Royal Fizz	99
Grenoble Ratafia	267
Grog	368

H

Hannibal Hamlin	162
Happy Moment	163
Heart's Content	164
Hip Liqueur	268
Hippocras	451
Holland Gin Cocktail	21
Holland's Pride	22
Holland Punch	369
Honey Wine à la Russe	507
Hong Kong Punch	38, 370
Hoppelpoppel, cold	371
hot	372
Hop Ratafia, English	269
Hot Wine	373, 374
à la Française	375
Hunters' Punch	376

I

Iced Lemonade	75
Punch	377
Imperial	76
Imperial Fizz	100
Punch	378
Invitation, The	166
Iva Liqueur	273

J

Jack Frost Whiskey Sour	1
Jamaica Rum à la Créole	167
John Collins	168
Judge, The	155
Juniper Cordial	274

K

Kajowsky	275
Kaleidoscope, The	169
Knickerbocker	170
Kümmel	276, 277
Kvass	495

L

Ladies' Delight	139
Great Favorite, The	171
Punch	379
hot	41
Lafayette Flip	148
Lait de Poule	39, 172
Lemonade, boiled	77
Gazeuse	78
Italian, hot	40
cold	54
Parfait	61
Seltzer	57
Soda	56
Strawberry	58

INDEX.

Lemon Bishop.............. 481
    Punch 380, 381
    Ratafia................. 278
        English......... 279
    Wine 508
Life-Prolonger, The........ 203
Lily Bouquet, The 124
Linden Blossom Bowl..... 452

M

Magenbitters 280, 281
Maiden's Kiss, A 173
Malinverno Punch......... 382
Manhattan Cocktail........ 23
    Cooler, The........... 174
    Punch 383
Maraschino 282
    Punch 384
Maurocordato 385
May Bowl........453, 454, 455
Mayflower, The 152
Mayor, The 175
Mecklenburg Punch....386, 387
Medical Drinks 226, 227
Melon Bishop 482
Militia Bowl 456
Milk Lemonade, English ... 72
    Punch, warm.......... 392
        English.388, 389, 390
        Finland 391
        Our 176
Mint Julep................. 178
    strained.......... 177
    Liqueur 283
Morning Delight 180
Mulberry Bishop.......... 483
My Hope 165

N

Nalifka 284
Nap, The 181
Nectar.................... 457
    in the English Style.458, 459
    Punch à l'Amérique.... 393
Negus 394, 395
Ne Plus Ultra............. 179
New Orleans Punch........ 182
' New York Herald, The ". 187
Nonpareil Liqueur......... 285
Norfolk Punch 396

Noyeau................... 286
Nuremberg Punch......... 397

O

Opal, The................. 25
Opal, Imperial............. 24
Opera, The 183
Orange Bishop 484
    Bowl 460
    Brandy, English....... 287
    Cardinal 461
    County Pride.......... 184
    County Punch......... 185
    Flower Ratafia 288
    Lemonade 79
        hot, with Brandy 42
    Liquor................ 289
    Punch 398
    Sherbet............... 80
        Turkish 81
    Wine 509
Orgeat.................... 462
Oriental Brandy Sour...... 5

P

Palate Tickler............. 186
Pansy Blossom, A......... 116
Parfait Amour.........290, 291
Paymaster, The 188
Peach Bishop.............. 485
    Bowl 463
    Brandy 316
    and Honey. 189
Pear Champagne 510
    Sherbet............... 82
Persian Sherbet 83
Persico 292, 293
Piazza 190
Pineapple Bishop.......... 486
    Julep................. 191
    Punch................. 192
Poem, The................ 193
Pomegranate Sherbet 84
Pope, The 464
Porter Bowl, English...... 465
    Flip 156
    Sangaree............. 194
Port Wine Punch.......... 400
    Sangaree........... 195
Pousse Café 200

Pousse l'Amour........... 198
Première, La............... 202
Preserver, The............ 26
Press, The................ 197
Primrose, The 196
Prince of Wales Punch..... 399
Promenade................. 199
Punch, American........... 322
    à la Bavaroise......... 404
    Burned, English....... 334
    Burning............... 333
    à la Crême............ 403
    à la Diable........... 401
    à l'Empereur.......... 402
    English.......356, 357, 358
    à la Ford............. 405
    à la Française.....406, 407
    à la Régence.......... 408
    à la Reine............ 409
    à la Romaine......410, 411
    à la Tyrolienne....... 412

Q

Queen of Night............ 204
Queen of Sheba............ 205
Quince Liquor.........294, 295
Quince Liquor, English.... 296
    Ratafia, French........ 297

R

Rainbow, The.............. 206
Raisin Sherbet, Turkish.... 85
    Wine.............511, 512
    in the Hebrew Style 513
Raspberry Bishop.......... 487
    Bowl.................. 467
    Lemonade.............. 86
    Lemonade with Wine... 55
    Punch 413, 414
    Ratafia................ 298
        French......... 299
    Wine.................. 514
        English......... 515
Red Wine Punch, hot...... 43
Reliever, The.............. 207
Reminder, The............. 208
Requiem, The.............. 211
Réséda Bowl............... 468
Reverie.................... 210
Rhine Wine Punch.....415, 416
Rhubarb Sherbet 87

Rice with Wine............ 488
Roman Punch.............. 209
Rose Ratafia............... 300
Rose-Hip Lemonade 88
Rosoglio................... 301
Royal Fizz................. 98
    Punch................. 417
Rum 302
    Flip................... 469
    Liquor................. 303
    Punch................. 418
Russian Punch............. 419

S

Saffron Liquor 304
Sangaree, West Indian...... 474
Sans Souci................. 212
Sapazeau................... 420
Scotch, Hot................ 44
    Delight 47
Senator, The............... 213
Shandy Gaff............... 214
Sherry Bowl............... 448
    Cobbler................ 93
    Filler.................. 146
    Flip................... 149
Sillabub.................... 470
    red.................... 471
Silver Fizz................. 96
Sitting Bull Fizz........... 103
Sloe Wine.................. 516
Snow Ball, The 215
Snow Flakes............... 421
Soda Cocktail 27
    Lemonade.............. 56
Sour à la Créole............ 2
Southern Cross, The....... 135
Spiced Rum, hot 50
Spiced Wine................ 517
Sporting Punch............. 422
Steel Punch................ 423
Stomach Essence 305
Strawberry Bishop......... 489
    Bowl................... 472
    Liquor................. 306
    Punch.................. 424
    Wine................... 518
"Sun, The"................ 216
Sure Relief, A............. 45
Swedish Punch............. 49
Sweet Bowl................. 473
Sweet Calamus Liquor..... 307

INDEX.

T

Tansy and Gin	218
Tea Punch, German	363, 364
"Texas Siftings" Punch	425
Tip-Top Sip	220
Tom and Jerry	219
Tom Collins	222
Tom Gin Cocktail	28

U

Uhles	426
United Service Punch	427
Usquebaugh, Irish	270, 271, 272

V

Vanilla Liquor	308, 309
Vermouth Cocktail	30
Vespetro	310
Vie Parisienne, La	221
Vin Brûlé	428
Violet Fizz	102
Violet Lemonade	59, 60

W

Walnut Liquor	311, 312
Washington Punch	429
Weeper's Joy, The	31
Whiskey	315
Cocktail	32
Cordial	313
Daisy	7
Frappé	154
Punch	430
Genuine	158
Sling	225
Sour	6
à la Guillaume	3
Whist	431
William's Summer Cooler	224
Wine Lemonade	89
Sherbet	90
Wischniak	519
"World's" Morning Delight	138
"World's" Pousse Café, The	201

Introduction and Cover Art Copyright 2008 -
All rights reserved.

TheDesignHouse
ISBN 1440449856

For regular updates on new reprint editions of
vinatge cocktail books,
vintage wine books,
vintage drinks books and
vintage cooking books
please visit

www.VintageCocktailBooks.com

Made in United States
North Haven, CT
21 September 2023